Updating
CLASSIC AMERICA

# RANCHES

# Updating
## CLASSIC AMERICA
# RANCHES

## Design Ideas for Renovating, Remodeling, and Building New

M. Caren Connolly
and Louis Wasserman

The Taunton Press

## The Taunton Press
Inspiration for hands-on living®

The Taunton Press, Inc., 63 South Main Street, PO Box 5506, Newtown, CT 06470-5506
e-mail: tp@taunton.com

Distributed by Publishers Group West

EDITOR: Peter Chapman
DESIGN AND LAYOUT: Lori Wendin
ILLUSTRATORS: Louis Wasserman and Elizabeth C. Wasserman, with original drawings of the period by
                Eugene Wasserman (p. v, 184, 200)
COVER PHOTOGRAPHER: Mark Heffron

*Updating Classic America: Ranches* was originally published in hardcover
in 2003 by The Taunton Press, Inc.

LIBRARY OF CONGRESS CATALOGING-IN-PUBLICATION DATA:
Connolly, M. Caren.
  Ranches : design ideas for renovating, remodeling, and building new /
M. Caren Connolly and Louis Wasserman.
      p. cm. -- (Updating classic America)
Includes index.
  ISBN-13 978-156158-437-6 hardcover
  ISBN-10 1-56158-437-1 hardcover
  ISBN-13 978-156158-741-4 paperback w/flaps
  ISBN-10 1-56158-741-9 paperback w/flaps
  1. Ranch houses--United States. 2. Architecture, Domestic--United
States. I. Wasserman, Louis. II. Title. III. Series.
NA7208 .C595 2003
728'.6--dc21

                2003008775

Printed in Singapore
10 9 8 7 6 5 4 3 2 1

The following brand names/manufacturers are trademarks: Tonka®

# Acknowledgments

To the memory of two terrific fathers:
*Eugene Wasserman,* a gifted artist and architect who excelled at the design of midcentury homes.

*John Scott Neprud,* a quiet intellectual, who raised a bunch of great kids in a series of Ranch homes.

OVER THE PAST TEN YEARS we have talked about writing a book on Ranches, a housing type that we both lived in as children and continue to be very excited about. We would like to thank all the people at The Taunton Press who made this book and the series, *Updating Classic America,* a reality: Jim Childs, Maria Taylor, Carolyn Mandarano, Paula Schlosser, Carol Singer, and Rosalind Wanke, all of whom, in addition to being extremely adept in the world of books and publishing, are exceedingly kind, smart, fun, and generous with their talents. We could not have written this book without our adept editor, Peter Chapman, who has the ability to combine pragmatism with delight. Special thanks go to Peter's ever-able assistant, Robyn Aitken, who manages to be both efficient and beneficent.

Minnesota architect Robert Gerloff was instrumental in getting *Ranches* up and running. He rounded up the majority of the homes in the book and, with writer Anna Kasabian, conducted the early interviews. Thank you both for an excellent head start.

The many photographers who provided the great images are listed on the facing page. We think it is fitting that such a ubiquitous housing type has finally been scrutinized through the lens of so many talented photographers. Sometimes ordinary objects need to be examined at close range in order to see their true worth clearly.

Finally, we are grateful to all the homeowners, their architects, designers, and contractors, who have clearly demonstrated their dedication to updating and preserving the legacy of Ranch homes as icons of American ingenuity and design into the new century.

# CONTENTS

# INTRODUCTION

RANCH HOUSES. These two words immediately conjure up a definitive image of American suburban homes, childhood stories, and mixed emotions. For a long time, Ranch houses were the homes everyone loved to hate. In the 1980s and '90s, America went on a wild residential building spree, resulting in ostentatious homes sitting alone on huge lots. In contrast, the closely knit, cul-de-sac Ranch neighborhoods of the '50s, '60s, and '70s began to look pretty good. They provide the opportunity for community many of us seek and that mini-estate living cannot provide.

Homebuyers are giving Ranch neighborhoods a second glance and a second chance. They are discovering that the Ranch style is a lot more flexible than anyone ever gave it credit for. The growing interest in Ranch homes is not about nostalgia, it's about the continuity of modern design principles: simplicity, functionality, and clarity. We think American residential design is now at the stage, like a child moving from adolescence to adulthood, when the frenzy for following the latest trend and impressing people is less important than it once was. Many house hunters today are coming to the realization that as one of the all-American housing types, the Ranch provides quality living experience over quantity of elaborate finishes, fussy details, and excess square footage. Opportunities to suit a variety of housing interests, from historic renovation to remaking the Ranch into a totally different style to building brand-new, can be found in most Ranch neighborhoods.

The Ranch has not only survived, it's on its way to timelessness.

# CHAPTER ONE

# RETURN OF THE RANCH

ABOVE, **The typical Ranch** elevation does not do a lot to quicken the pulse of the homebuyer. The low profile and simple exterior treatment belie the opportunity for personal expression on the interior.

FACING PAGE, **The Ranch house,** with its signature floor-to-ceiling windows, links the outdoors with the inside. Breaking down artificial barriers was one of the hallmarks of Ranch design; rooms were designed to have multiple uses to reflect a family's changing mood.

RANCH HOUSES ARE EVERYWHERE, from Maine to California, in small towns, in the suburbs of large cities, and in the distant countryside. No house type is more ubiquitous in the landscape, and none triggers such mixed emotions. Unlike vernacular Bungalows and Cape Cods, Ranches are so common as to be almost invisible. Few of us acknowledge that they have a place in the history of American design. The Ranch's reputation is complicated by the fact that these houses symbolize different things to different generations.

To the veterans returning from World War II, the Ranch house was an enduring symbol of the American Dream—the wish to marry and raise a family in their own houses, on their own plots of land, in safe and prosperous communities. Flush with VA loans, they bought millions of Ranches, and between 1945 and 1970 the style become the most commonly built in America.

**Typical of many Ranch** neighborhoods, you can barely see the house for the trees. Increasingly, neighborhoods with mature plantings are gaining in value, and the large back yards have more than enough room for adding on.

The Ranch meant something else to the children who grew up in these homes. For this generation—the baby boomers—the style symbolized the rigid complacency and conformity of the times which many boomers struggled to change during the ideological battles of the 1960s. After a 30-year building spree, both the appetite for Ranch homes and the landscape were saturated.

But the Ranch's popularity is rising once again. Home buyers have come to appreciate both the subtle appeal of these straightforward homes and the settled suburban neighborhoods in which they tend to be found. Ironically, home seekers who swore they would never return to cul-de-sac living find themselves cruising the curving lanes of Ranch neighborhoods looking for "For Sale" signs and rediscovering why these homes were so immensely popular the first time around.

## Ranch Appeal

Although "chic" and "fashionable" are not words often used to describe the Ranch, these houses have a lot going for them—convenient location, quality construction, and a well-conceived design. What's more, Ranches fit the casual lifestyle that most homeowners are comfortable with today.

Americans are spending more time at their jobs and commuting, meaning fewer hours at home, and in an indirect way this has made the Ranch more appealing. Most houses of this style were built in the inner ring of postwar suburbs, conveniently linked by highways with both older city centers and "edge city" office parks in the new, distant suburbs. Ranch neighborhoods also benefit from mature trees, decent schools, and active community groups—factors that just can't be built into a neighborhood overnight.

Ranch houses were mass-produced using assembly-line techniques mastered in building bombers and tanks during World War II. This might suggest that they were shoddily built; after all, there isn't much quality *visible* in a Ranch house. An Arts and Crafts Bungalow, in contrast, is bursting with built-in bookcases and quartersawn oak trim. But Ranches were built with care—their quality happens to be concealed within the walls and floors. For example, floors were typically framed with 2x10 Douglas fir joists, free from knots and blemishes. Today, it's difficult to buy clear Douglas fir even for such finish work as cabinetry. The same quality of materials can be found throughout the house. The advantages aren't just aesthetic. Solidly constructed houses age better and are easier to remodel and add onto.

The current trend toward simplifying day-to-day living and spending more time enjoying friends, family,

**Tile, woodwork, and the views** outside are as important in the updating of Ranch houses as they were in the originals.

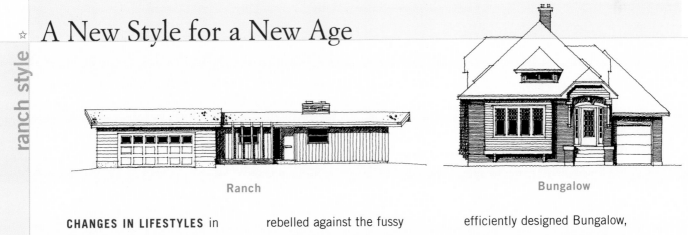

ranch style

# A New Style for a New Age

Ranch

Bungalow

**CHANGES IN LIFESTYLES** in the post–World War II era were reflected in changes in the traditional form of the house. Just as the Bungalow had rebelled against the fussy Victorian, the Ranch, with its low, rambling silhouette, was a reaction to the boxlike and compressed Bungalow. Unlike the efficiently designed Bungalow, the Ranch expressed freedom from boundaries, both physical and social.

**The renovation of** this 1960s split-level Ranch demonstrates that it is possible to create theater and excitement in a housing type that has the reputation for being dull. The suspended metal catwalk shows the same interest in industrial design and prefabricated building parts as the innovative Ranch designs of the1950s.

neighbors, and hobbies has strong parallels with the lifestyle of Ranch dwellers of the 1950s. Those who grew up in predominantly Ranch neighborhoods can probably recall summer nights when kids gathered at the end of the street and played kick the can while their parents gathered around a brick barbecue pit and talked the night away. The current generation of Ranch owners shares other lifestyle interests with the first generation, namely an intrigue with technology and innovation. The rec room and the kitchen in early Ranch homes were designed around a new generation of electronics and appliances. Today, plasma screens need wall space just as console TVs needed a built-in; surround-sound ceiling speakers replace High-Fidelity floor

# The "Trade Secrets" House

**ON 5 JANUARY, 1953,** *Life* magazine devoted a special issue to the American economy. The cover article, which pictured a family of four in their new home, featured "the U.S. home builders' best buy . . . the $15,000 'Trade Secrets' house."

The Trade Secrets house, designed by the National Association of Home Builders, was a direct response to consumer demand for "a good looking skillfully engineered house." Since the end of World War II, home building had changed from a craft to an industry, where assembly-line techniques that were applied to building were guarded jealously as if they were "trade secrets." Those secrets were revealed in a well-designed ranch

home with three bedrooms, 1½ baths, and a fireplace in 1,340 sq. ft. of open plan living designed with flexibility. This was a home that could be built anywhere in the United States for $15,000. It was also a Ranch home with all the typical identifying hallmarks.

Windows, doors, walls, trusses, siding, and sheathing were uniformly sized and partly preassembled so that they could be integrated efficiently. Walls were framed on an economical slab on grade and then tilted up and the windows and doors inserted. What we accept today as the norm was first demonstrated in the Trade Secrets house of 1953. Expansion options were numerous—and well

they should have been, because this efficient plan was tight. With no basement, even the numerous storage walls weren't sufficient for American consumers, and the bedrooms were tiny.

Short on space, but high on design and efficiency, this fresh-faced contractor contemporary, complete with its Herman Miller furniture, was an overnight sensation.

**Folding screens and curtains** were a device used in 1950s Ranch homes to create a variety of rooms within one large space. Fifty years later, the device still works. Movable translucent glass walls (at right) in this Atlanta home can reconfigure the room in an instant. Recessed ceiling lighting changes the mood in the evening.

speakers; and microwave ovens join double-wall ovens in competition for wall space in kitchens.

The simple geometry and detailing of the Ranch style allow ultimate flexibility for homeowners to put their own aesthetic stamp on the house. One of the main selling points for the early Ranch was that it did not conform to any one style or period. A major reason Ranch homes are gaining in popularity today is that a "blank canvas" lets owners explore their own creative ideas on how to remodel an aging house.

# Ranch Hallmarks

The classic Ranch is a rectangular or L-shaped house whose low-pitched roof caps an open, free-flowing plan. The house is typically long, narrow, and low to the ground, with a strong emphasis on the horizontal. The orientation of the house and the low roof, which acts as a sun-control device, were originally intended to promote energy efficiency. Large expanses of glass window walls allow the sun to penetrate deep into the open plan. In addition, the generous use of glass expands the visual limits, breaking down conventional boundaries. While most Ranches are one story, split-levels accommodate the house to sloping sites.

## EXTERIOR HALLMARKS

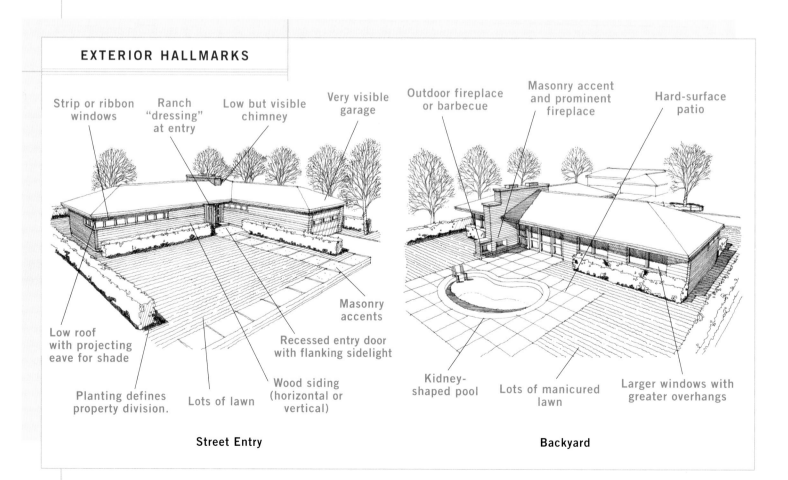

Street Entry

Backyard

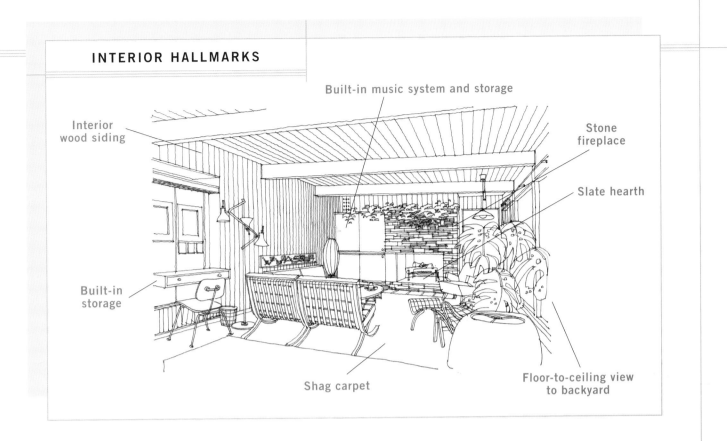

## INTERIOR HALLMARKS

Interior wood siding

Built-in music system and storage

Stone fireplace

Slate hearth

Built-in storage

Shag carpet

Floor-to-ceiling view to backyard

One often-heard complaint about the Ranch style is that the fronts of the houses ignore the street. Early Ranch homeowners treasured their privacy—the homes were built for family enjoyment, not to enhance the public street—and porches were considered old-fashioned and too public. One exception was the front door, which typically expressed the individual personality and hospitality of the house, often with accents of bright colors and large sidelights.

The Ranch interior emphasizes casual, family-centered living. And as forbidding as many of the street exteriors appear, Ranch homes, more successfully than any other housing style, seize the opportunity to integrate indoor and outdoor living, with connections from major living spaces directly to the outdoors. A Ranch yard is conceived of as a garden that can be viewed as a feature from within the house, both day and night. Residential night lighting is an idea that developed right along with Ranch style.

The open plan of the Ranch, with a living room that accommodates multiple activities, captures the

**The breakfast bar,** connecting the kitchen to the other living spaces, is as popular in the contemporary Ranch as it was in the 1950s classic, emphasizing the easy informality of the Ranch style.

ABOVE, **A strong connection** between indoor and outdoor living is one of the defining hallmarks of Ranch style. Here, the windowsill of the picture window to the backyard is low to the ground to enhance the feeling of connectivity.

FACING PAGE, **New or remodeled** Ranch homes employ the principles of the first wave of Ranch building: open plan, connection to nature, natural materials, exposed structure, reduced maintenance, and expression of personal interests.

rhythm and flow of contemporary American living. Early Ranches combined dining and living rooms, often separated only by a low built-in credenza, anticipating the demise of the formal dining room. Another common combination is the kitchen/laundry room, which is a feature highly sought after in today's residential market.

## BEST-KEPT SECRETS

The best-kept secret about Ranch homes is that they were built with quality materials and designed with flexibility and additions in mind. Built at a time when both the population and the economy were growing, the idea of planning for expansion was a natural. Most early Ranch plans include notations for future conversion of the garage into a family room or a work room, for adding a master bedroom wing, or for converting a carport into a garage. The first Ranch owners really did look at their opportunities as limitless—they just didn't believe they had to have it all at once. This is one idea

ABOVE AND BELOW, **This brand-new Ranch** built in Wisconsin continues the tradition of carrying an exterior stone wall into the interior fireplace wall, a common design device in 1950s Ranches.

that is gaining in appeal for today's more deliberate (and economically savvy) homeowners.

## HIDDEN TREASURES

The concept of planned obsolescence did not exist in the 1940s and '50s. Homeowners fixed things rather than replaced them. Interior finishes in Ranch homes—linoleum, cork, wood, and slate floors—were built to last. Interior and exterior walls were commonly sheathed in materials that are now on the endangered species list: mahogany, teak, pecky cypress, and old-growth cedar. While these now priceless (and no longer available) materials may be covered up by latex paint or wall-to-wall carpeting, the ordinary Ranch house could have a wealth of quality materials that need only be revealed to restore their original glory. You may also be surprised to find that the original heating and cooling units are still functioning, although you'd be well advised to replace them with more energy-efficient units.

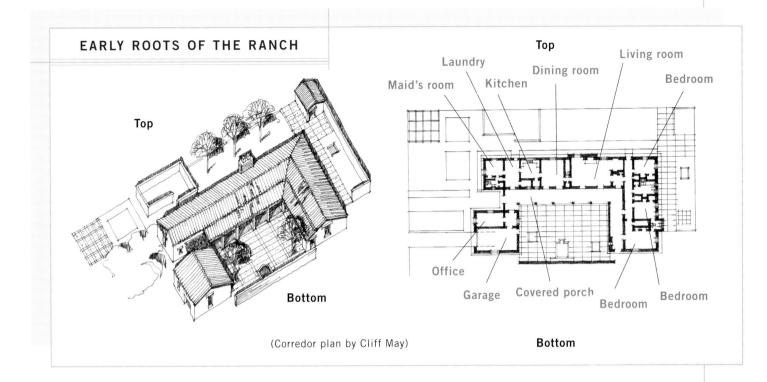

Top

Bottom

(Corredor plan by Cliff May)

Top

Laundry
Maid's room
Kitchen
Dining room
Living room
Bedroom

Office
Garage
Covered porch
Bedroom
Bedroom

Bottom

### SUBTLE STYLING

At first glance, Ranch homes may appear to lack the ornamental detailing so admired in Bungalows or Colonial-style homes. The beauty of the Ranch home lies in the subtle manner in which details are not ornamental, but essential. Following the ideals of the Modern movement in architecture, applied decoration was considered old-fashioned. Instead, inside and out, the walls, floors, and ceiling were all components of a well-worked composition. The common Ranch design device of carrying the exterior brick or stone wall into the interior fireplace wall, providing texture and color and ease of maintenance, clearly illustrates this concept (see the photos on the facing page).

## Origins of the Ranch

Most postwar Ranches were family homes designed and constructed by developers and builders, and they represented such everyday values as pragmatism and modesty. Nevertheless, the style draws on ideas of the foremost architects of the 1900s, including Frank Lloyd Wright and even the theorists behind the cutting-edge Modernist movement. Today it's difficult to think of Ranches as "bold" and "modern," simply because they are so familiar.

### CLIFF MAY AND THE *RANCHO*

The Ranch is a truly American housing style. Like so many cultural innovations in this country, the roots of the Ranch can be traced back to California. In the late 1940s and early '50s, much of what we know about the California lifestyle was shaped, influenced, fostered, and publicized by the various publications of *Sunset* magazine, and in particular by the work of a young California designer called Cliff May, the unsung hero of the modern Ranch house. In 1946, at the height of the postwar housing boom, *Sunset* and May published *Western Ranch Houses*, a best-seller that outlined the ideas of the Ranch house and showed dozens of examples. It is the book that launched the Ranch house revolution.

With deep eaves, a low-pitched roof, and a strong connection between house and environment, the influence of Frank Lloyd Wright's Prairie houses is evident in this newly constructed Midwestern Ranch.

May looked for inspiration to the traditional adobe *ranchos* of Colonial California. These homesteads had been built by Spanish-speaking cattle ranchers from Mexico and were ideally suited to the benign California climate. *Ranchos* in turn had their roots in the Roman atrium house and essentially turned their backs on the street and hot weather by providing a shaded and cooler inner open court, which was surrounded by a continuous column-lined veranda called a *corredor* (see the drawing on p. 15). This inner courtyard can be thought of as the original family room, an informal place where everyone could gather. These historic Ranches hugged the ground because they were built simply of local and natural materials, many without foundations, directly on hardened ground.

May's designs were hybrids, combining the deep overhanging eaves and expansive floor plans of the *ranchos* with the shake roofs and wood siding introduced to California by settlers from the East. His interiors were woodsy and self-consciously Western, displaying their rustic roots while exemplifying many of the

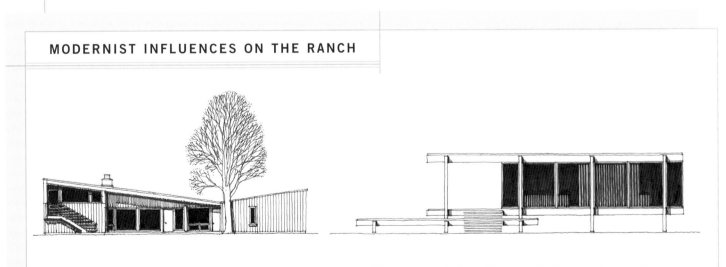

## MODERNIST INFLUENCES ON THE RANCH

Marcel Breuer's MOMA House, New York City

Mies van der Rohe's Farnsworth House, Plano, Illinois

Modern movement characteristics of horizontal lines and convenient living in a style that was more open and versatile than that of most American homes of that time.

## FRANK LLOYD WRIGHT AND PRAIRIE PRECEDENTS

The second major influence in Ranch design is the residential work of Frank Lloyd Wright. If you compare the hallmarks of the Ranch to those of Wright's Midwestern-derived Prairie homes of the 1910s and his later single-story homes of the '30s, '40s, and '50s, you'll see that they share an open floor plan, an easy flow from inside to out, use of natural local materials, expansive use of glazing, and ground-hugging horizontal lines. The use of zoned wings for the different functions of living, sleeping, work, and garage is common to both the Prairie and the ranch.

Wright's ideas about site planning, truth in materials, and organic architecture were realized in widely-published and popularized homes across the county from the 1930s to the 1950s. His first trip to Japan in 1915 and subsequent trips proved fertile sources of ideas, among them the inspiration for the open plan.

Wright's creative application of his well-developed design philosophy formatively influenced the California Ranch and the Trade Secrets house, and contributed overall to the evolution of what we know as the Ranch.

## MODERN FOR THE MASSES

Unlikely as it may seem, the humble Ranch introduced Modern design to Middle America. When Walter Gropius, Marcel Breuer, and Mies van der Rohe came to the United States in the 1930s from Germany, they introduced the International Style. Settling in Boston, Gropius built a number of handsome homes of local wood and stone that prefigured the Ranch contemporaries. Nearby, Breuer employed split-faced fieldstone, laminated beams, and expansive glass in a series of graceful homes that married the International Style to the American housing vernacular. And Mies van der Rohe's Farnsworth house, with walls of floor-to-ceiling glass, was the ultimate expression of a house that encouraged indoor-outdoor connections.

These 1940s homes were covered extensively in architectural magazines of the time. In 1949, the

Museum of Modern Art in New York constructed in its sculpture garden a modest Breuer-designed home for a middle-income family that featured "indoor and out-door zones" and was programmed for future expansion. In the Midwest, the Keck and Keck brothers, who were well established before the European invasion, continued to build their own American interpretation of the International Style applied to Ranch-like examples. On the West Coast, German expatriates like Richard Neutra and R.M. Schindler built and extolled the virtues of modern housing and further laid the groundwork for the contemporary Ranch.

**Ranch home exteriors** were typified by an emphasis on front door, to express hospitality. The rest of the front elevation intentionally presented a fairly blank façade to the street, not to be forbidding, but to heighten the drama of passing through an opaque wall to a transparent interior that revealed a private landscape.

# A Classic Contemporary

While it may be hard for most people to imagine a Historic Register plaque appearing on a Ranch house, it is happening. Just as a car that survives the crusher for 25 years is eligible for collector plates, a 50-year-old building can acquire historic status. Clearly, not all Ranch homes deserve to be preserved, but there is a growing awareness of the cultural importance of this style, and groups are forming to save architecturally and culturally significant examples. Let's look now at a house in Atlanta that has been restored in the lively spirit of the period, if not to the letter of preservation standards.

### SEEING THE POTENTIAL

The real estate agent was hesitant to show Debra the house, which had been on the market for two years. But when Debra saw the aging 1950s Ranch, she recognized possibilities that no one else had noticed. She knew that restoring the house to its full potential would be both time- and money-consuming, but the background knowledge she'd gained from her research into the Ranch style told her this house would be worth it. And it would be a joy to realize her dream of having a house worthy of her collection of midcentury furniture. The house also earns its keep; it is such a classic restoration that both print and television commercials have found it desirable as a stage set.

One of the hallmarks of Ranch style is that the homes are designed to accommodate future expansion. It was not unusual for early Ranch home owners to live for a year or two in a finished (or semifinished) basement while they completed building the "real" home above them. And while Debra did want to restore the home to 1950s standards, we're not sure she wanted

**The original kitchen** was daylit only by the skylight. The present owner removed a pantry and opened up an entire wall to counter-to-ceiling windows. She was careful to choose slider windows that are compatible with the 1950s aesthetic of the home. Abundant recessed can lighting in both the ceiling and the exterior soffit ensures that the kitchen is well lit at night.

## FLOOR PLAN

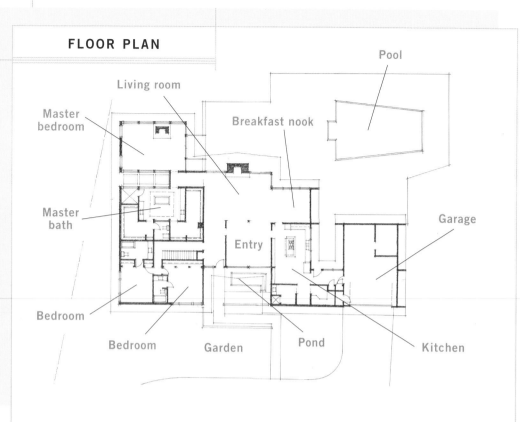

Pool

Living room

Master bedroom

Breakfast nook

Master bath

Entry

Garage

Bedroom

Bedroom

Garden

Pond

Kitchen

FACING PAGE, **Natural woods** and functional hardware and appliances are all trademarks of Ranch kitchens. Convenience was a key word in kitchen design vocabulary. For the first time in American residential design, the kitchen was conferred equal status with the other living spaces.

BELOW, **The new addition** was designed to match the integrity of the original house. The floor-to-ceiling windows in the bathroom include the garden as part of the experience. As in the remodeled kitchen, careful attention is paid to interior and exterior lighting.

to replicate the 1950s basement living experience. But she did; due to age and neglect, parts of the house had to be gutted down to the studs to repair structural defects. Shiny wood floors replaced terrazzo floors, new windows were a must, and new lighting, air-conditioning, and heating were all installed. And while she was at it, Debra redid the kitchen and added a master bedroom and bath.

### HALLMARKS OF THE STYLE

At 5,000 sq. ft., this home is two to three times larger than most Ranches built in the 1960s and '70s. The pedigree is revealed in the expression of each of the Ranch hallmarks. Privacy from the street was of paramount importance in the design of the early Ranches; here, the two wing walls of the house embrace the set-back glass entrance. Not forbidding,

but welcoming, you can see all the way through the house to the landscape beyond from the front entry. Ranch homes express the epitome of hospitality and relaxed entertaining. The red front door hints that the stuffiness of a lifestyle symbolized by a nine-panel door is not what this house is about. Doors of Ranch homes were and still are painted bright colors as a simple way to express individuality.

Typical of most Ranches, Debra's home is one story of living space, but prefabricated laminated wood beams and exposed cedar roof decks allow for longer spans and greater clearance. During the first wave of Ranch building, one-and-a-half- or two-story living rooms were highly sought after. There was a practical reason: Many communities denied building permits for single-story homes, fearing an invasion of cheaply built postwar one-story builder housing. Homes needed to be one-and-a-half or two stories in appearance, if not function, to gain building permit approval.

In Debra's home, the exposed ceiling beams are clearly visible through the windows as roof structure. This inside-outside connection carries through in the structure of the home as well as to inside-outside views throughout, and Debra was careful to continue the hallmark in the new addition.

## MATERIAL DECISIONS

Debra was keen to maintain design purity, but she drew the line at the wood paneling, which was very popular with some 1950s architects. Most of today's homeowners feel, as Debra did, that the dark tones of the wood paneling soak up too much light, and opt for wall surfaces that reflect the light and show off art more effectively. (Not that all original Ranch homes were paneled; some

# Ranch Lighting

**WITH THE HALLMARKS** of an open plan and large windows, abundant natural light streaming through the public zone became a major attraction for the Ranch. Artificial lighting was needed only at night. At first, lighting designs responded stylistically with various fixtures designed to be seen from all around the open plan as modern objects that supplemented the abundant natural light. Many of the original high-style light fixtures pictured in 1950s interiors have become collectors' items, and some are still in production, like the artichoke fixture by Poul Henningsen shown in the photo above.

In time, contemporary designers saw the need to design with different types of artificial light, including diffused and indirect, and to emphasize the surface lit rather than the fixture. The popularity of darker interior finishes called for more light.

The 1960s saw the adaptation of theatrical track lighting to residential uses, in particular the Ranch. Versatile and attractive, track systems come in conventional 1-in. track, undulating flat bands, and stretched paired bare cable. The exposed track can be mounted directly to a ceiling or suspended, the perfect complement to the Ranch open plan, especially where beam, deck, and track light fixture can all be exposed.

Whereas 1950s cold cathode or neon was used for linear and indirect lighting, fiber optics or low-voltage "ropes" may be used today. Recessed light fixtures accented in soffited areas of the '50s Ranch and are now available in sizes ranging from 8-in.-diameter energy-saving fluorescent to 3-in.-diameter low-voltage, low-clearance units.

architects and designers in the 1950s were excited by new concepts of interior lighting and chose wall finishes that minimized glare, unified the spaces, and reflected artificial and natural light.)

The original dining room and living room floors were terrazzo, which was very much in vogue during the 1950s (often with radiant heating). Again, Debra weighed in on the side of prevailing taste; the satin-finish maple flooring is quieter, easier to clean, and warmer in appearance than the terrazzo. As with many of the decisions Debra made, the principles of the Ranch are intact but the materials and colors have changed.

The skylights in the kitchen are original to the home. Contrary to the common complaint that builder Ranches have small, dark kitchens, the true Ranch style has an efficient kitchen; it is intended to be the working heart of the home. Views to the outdoors, natural light, and integration with the active living spaces of the home are all qualities that Ranch owners treasure. Other than the skylight, very little remains of the original kitchen. A pantry was removed to open up a wall for counter-to-ceiling slider windows that reinforce the

**The owner's collection** of midcentury furniture fits perfectly in the living room. Early Ranch houses were designed to reflect the wide-ranging interests and tastes of their owners, and mixing old and new was very much a Ranch design principle.

inside-outside connection. A built-in wall of cherry wood cabinets serves as room divider (very hot in the 1950s) and provides the storage that was lost when the pantry was removed. The flush doors and simple hardware continue the modern theme. The granite-topped island is not a standard of Ranch kitchen design, but the double wall oven most certainly is.

## COURTYARD LIVING

Expressing a new spirit of freedom was one of the goals of early Ranch designers. They did this in a variety of ways, one of which was to create the illusion of space with floor-to-ceiling window walls. War-time technology brought us pressure-sealed windows, and mass production made large windows affordable, even for the middle class.

Hearkening back to Ranch roots, the California courtyard house was the epitome of privacy and good ventilation. The new bathing room in Debra's home borrows a page from that book. Taking a bath in this room is both private and connected to nature—a great way to begin a work day! The slate flooring and square

ceramic tiles of the bath surround would not be out of place in an original Ranch, while the uplighting, the clerestory, and the skylight create the illusion of a much taller room.

Debra's house is a great example of the "Houses for One" concept extolled in the design magazines of the time, "with an emphasis on privacy and personal taste." The master bedroom, with its slate-faced fireplace, window walls, and seating area (see the photo on the facing page), illustrates the Ranch credo that "building now and decorating later" was considered old-fashioned. Mood lighting, wall-to-wall carpet, built-in furnishings, and limiting window treatments to sun control (Debra installed an electrical shade system) were celebrated as the modern way of furnishing a home.

# Ranch Options

Ranch houses were designed for the fantasy '50s family: a hard-working husband with a stay-at-home wife, 2.3 kids, and a dog. Today, a considerably smaller percentage of households fits that description. In their place are

blended families created by remarrying, "empty nesters" whose children have left home, couples without children, single adults with roommates and single adults living alone. The list of possible variations is endless, and each household wants something different. Fortunately, the Ranch may be the easiest of styles to remodel or add on to. With its simple roof form, straightforward framing system, relatively modern foundation, and generous yard, the Ranch is a remodeler's dream. Let's look at the options.

## WITHIN THE WALLS

We'll start with a confession: Even we find the majority of Ranch exteriors hard to love. But remember, it's the inner character that counts. The long horizontal profile of the Ranch style can present formidable design challenges. In addition, two of the hallmark Ranch exterior materials, stone and brick, are virtually impossible to alter without incurring major expense and possibly compromising the integrity of the structure. The good news is that many of these Ranches were built so solidly that nonstructural walls usually can be removed to reconfigure rooms without worry that the house will

# What's in a Name?

**THE WORD *RANCH*** conjures up different images depending on what part of the country you live in. Out West and in the Southwest, people think of a Ranch as a farm or "spread" with cattle, a pickup truck, and lots of acres (think the Reagan Ranch, for one presidential example).

For the rest of us, a Ranch is a more modest dwelling, a single-story structure—or so it usually appears from the street. Aside from a bit of dressing up at the front door, what we like to call "Ranch Dressing," the Ranch reserves much of its architectural oomph for its more private back yard.

A split-level Ranch (also known as a Raised Ranch in some parts of the country) typically has a grade-entry foyer with a stair that leads up half a flight to bedrooms and down half a fight to garage and recreation room. Living, dining, and kitchen are at grade or half a level up. A "split Ranch" is typically one story, with the master bedroom suite separated at the entry from the rest of the house for privacy.

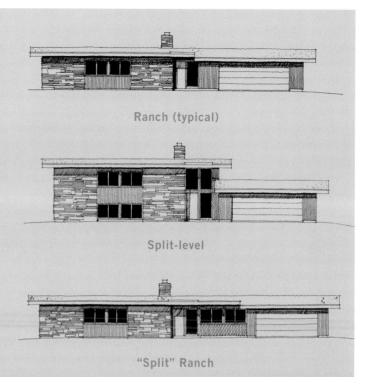

Ranch (typical)

Split-level

"Split" Ranch

One other term you may come across: In the upper Midwest, especially in Minnesota, Ranches are colloquially called "ramblers," probably because of their low, ground-hugging tendency to sprawl across the site. In Wisconsin, that term is reserved for very old cars.

fall down. Take heart—a homely exterior often masks the possibilities for a stunning interior; chapter 2 illustrates what homeowners can achieve when they intentionally look for houses to gut and start from the studs to create a brand-new interior.

## COMPLETING THE PLAN

Another confession: As much as today's homebuyer may admire the well-engineered structure and the quality finishes of the Ranch style, most of them lack the square footage and amenities to satisfy today's family. As we show in chapter 3, this is actually an asset of the Ranch. Because it is small, it is one of the most affordable housing styles. And since Ranch lots are typically quite large, adding a wing (or two) onto the one-story home will generally not be a problem. And building onto a one-story Ranch house poses fewer design challenges than adding a story to other styles, such as the Bungalow or Cape Cod. Because the majority of additions will likely be in the deep back yard, the front of the home can maintain its stylistic hallmarks, even if the addition is radically different.

## COMPLETE TRANSFORMATIONS

Ranch neighborhoods are prized for their mature landscapes, sense of neighborhood, existing infrastructure, and convenient location to workplace and quality schools, but the Ranch style is not everyone's idea of a

ABOVE, **Ranch homes** were designed to be added onto, typically in the backyard. Early designers anticipated that as families grew in size or in interests the original square footage might not be sufficient.

LEFT, **Most Ranch homes** of the 1950s do need to be updated. This new metal-and-wood stair rail creates a sculptural focal point while visually connecting what had been two separate rooms. The expressed pipe columns provide the needed structure to replace the original bearing wall. Rather than hide the structure, the designer integrated it into the design vocabulary of the new stair.

dream house. More than any other housing style, the Ranch elicits either a strong positive or an equally strong negative response. In chapter 4, you'll find examples of homeowners who took advantage of the structure of obsolete (and in some cases downright ugly) Ranch houses in great locations to create a completely different architectural style. Every home in this chapter built on the bones of the original house, a form of sustainable building practice. The transformations run the gamut from an English garden home to cutting-edge "Blob" architecture.

## NEW CONSTRUCTION

By their sheer numbers, the first generation of children raised in Ranch homes has had a huge impact on trends, fashion, and the economy during the past 50 years. As baby boomers age, they are finding that the one-story, open-plan, easy-to-maintain Ranch appeals to their strong sense of independence. And while

Ranch homes may be considered too small for families, these smaller homes are perfect for singles or empty nesters who enjoy visitors but want to downsize. For the 50-somethings who prefer to remain active in the communities they worked in and enjoy the cultural benefits, their retirement home is likely to be a new Ranch home rather than a condo on a beach.

Chapter 5 shows two examples of new construction; one is a contemporary home built for a couple in a rural setting and the other is a reinterpretation of the Prairie style Ranch, built only a few miles from some of Frank Lloyd Wright's most representational residential work. While the two homes look quite different, they both use Ranch hallmarks, expressing contemporary lifestyles and integrating today's technology.

As the Ranch gets a new, appreciative look from a new generation of homeowners, there's a need for positive examples of what can go right with a renovation, a remodel, or new construction. The following pages show houses from across the country, some modest and others more extensive. In each case, the homeowners have felt some affection for the unadorned style and used the Ranch's agreeable simplicity as the basis for a three-dimensional improvisation.

ABOVE, **In true Ranch spirit,** the owner and the architect of this Chicago home, which was originally a split-level Ranch, were excited about working with new materials and technological innovations to create a home that reflected the personality of the family.

FACING PAGE, **Whether the original Ranch** had a rectangular-, L-, or a U-shaped footprint, it readily accepts additions, horizontally, vertically, or both. Many communities encourage large additions, because they increase property values and the tax base.

# CHAPTER TWO

# RANCH REVIVAL

ABOVE, **It's difficult** to find anyone who loves the exterior of the ubiquitous 1960s to 1970s Ranch, even people who love Ranch neighborhoods and the home's flexible floor plan. Most Ranch owners accept the exterior as a given and expend their time, energy, thought, and money on interior renovations.

FACING PAGE, **Distance, diversity and water** are the three required elements for a beautiful vista. This California ranch has all three, fully visible from the major living spaces of the house.

A NY REMODELING PROJECT REQUIRES careful planning, some dreaming, and a well-worked-out budget. If the house you bought, or the one you are thinking about buying, is the right size, in the right neighborhood, and affordable, your major concern is more than likely how livable the interior spaces are or can be. If you are living in a predominantly Ranch neighborhood, chances are the houses on your street share similar exterior characteristics. "Curb appeal" is not a hot buzzword for Ranch real estate. In many Ranch neighborhoods, because the back yard is the "front door" for family and friends, the street façade is private. In chapter 3, we'll show examples of Ranches that have been radically renovated; this chapter focuses on more modest and largely interior renovations.

**Early Ranch houses** treated the street as the service entry; it was the domain of the automobile. The back yard was as open as the front was closed.

## Ready for an Update

The 1950s, '60s, and '70s were the boom time for Ranch development. Ranches were primarily conceived of as homes for young families, and it's likely that many Ranches currently on the market have had only one or two owners. Human nature being what it is, the fewer the owners, the less the interior décor has been changed. The roof has probably been resurfaced, the brick tuck-pointed, and the gutters replaced, but chances are a shag rug or two may remain, the color scheme might be straight from the '70s, and there may be a wealth of dark wood paneling lining the walls of the major living spaces.

But don't despair, cosmetic changes are more easily (and economically) achieved than sweeping structural changes. It's likely that wood floors are lying securely protected under that shag carpeting. Painting is one of the easiest ways to dramatically claim a space as your own, and drywall is an inexpensive way to finish walls (and the lighter, smoother wall finishes will instantly make the rooms look 30 percent larger). Given that kitchens are usually remodeled every 15 years, the home you are buying is doubtless due for an update anyway.

**In some parts** of the South and the West, even very modest Ranch homes have in-ground swimming pools. This California house is certainly a cut above modest and has fully embraced the idea of indoor-outdoor living. How many outdoor rooms have seating for eight and an exterior chandelier?

# ☆ Updating the Kitchen

**TODAY ANY KITCHEN** over seven years old is ripe for renovation. New Ranch owners may be motivated by a need to change appliances, colors, or finishes; to add new labor-saving appliances; or simply to remake the kitchen in their own personal style. It's also the perfect opportunity to update electrical service, improve efficiency of layout, and add more counter space, all in the name of revising yesterday's efficient kitchen to accommodate today's sociable kitchen.

The Ranch kitchen was probably the first to employ the commonly accepted formula of the work triangle. According to this formula, the sum of distances from refrigerator to stove to sink and back should not exceed 23 ft. or be less than 12 ft. Each side of the triangle should be more than 4 ft. and less than 9 ft. Even with all the added labor-saving devices (which usually aren't), this rule holds true.

Unless your Ranch kitchen is constricted by a basement stair, you probably have enough room to revise or expand your layout. Because appliance sizes and mechanical services haven't changed that much, you can replace appliances and update countertop and floor finishes. If more space is needed, you might expand into the living room, dining room, or pantry—or possibly pop out into your back yard. A new buffet adds counter or eating space and provides a functional and visual connection to your dining or living area. Wall openings can be cut between spaces to provide visual expansion without the need to actually add space.

## TASTES CHANGE OVER TIME

One thing that makes residential design so interesting is that it reflects the popular culture of the time. Every decade has its particular design emphasis. Some designs are more enduring than others. We still haven't come up with a meaningful architectural definition for the 1980s term "great room," nor have we figured out what a "cathedral ceiling" has to do with residential architecture. During the Ranch decades, definitions were clearer—at times, the ardent architectural theory of modern design read like a manifesto. Emphasis was on personal expression, individual happiness, and ridding the house of wasted space. Today, we want a bit of luxury in our busy lives, so bathrooms and kitchens are high on the list of Ranch remodels.

Ranch bathrooms were larger than Bungalow or Colonial bathrooms but the emphasis was still on efficiency. Today's bathroom industry has been creatively developing products that can transform any bathroom into a spa. Galleylike Ranch kitchens and the disappearing formal dining room foreshadowed the mass movement of women into the workplace. Today, kitchens rank as the most popular room where family and

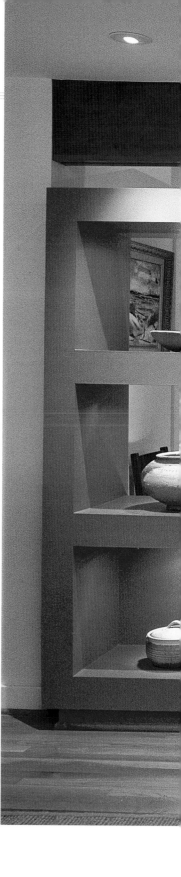

**Extra-deep whirlpool tubs** in a variety of shapes and styles provide at-home luxury. The glass block allows an abundance of shimmering light to filter through without compromising modesty.

friends gather, and some families are also welcoming back the formal dining room. The remodels that follow in this chapter are faithful to the midcentury originals, but they also reflect the latest in contemporary trends.

## Expect the Unexpected

Part of the challenge of remodeling a Ranch is dealing with the experimental nature of Ranch construction. "Hmmm, that's interesting" are three words you don't want to hear from a contractor. But as anyone who's ever lived through a remodeling project will tell you, it is guaranteed there will be at least one surprise during the "exploration" part of the process.

To ward off as many unfortunate surprises as possible, always ask sellers if they have a set of drawings for

**When it comes to lighting,** Ranch rooms are a lot like art galleries: They provide a neutral background to best show off whatever is being displayed. During the early Ranch era, designers were excited about lighting design, both natural and artificial. This home combines a traditional pendant light with recessed ceiling cans to wash the dining room with light. The art collection is housed in cabinets with built-in spotlights, while the hall is bathed in the glow of hidden indirect lighting in a coved ceiling.

## Deconstructing the Ranch

**ONE OF THE ADVANTAGES** of updating a Ranch is that much of its structural information is in plain view. A visit to your basement or attic will reveal a lot about the house and help inform you whether partitions can be removed, relocated, or added. But remember, no structural change should be made without the advice of an architect or engineer.

A typical Ranch floor (with a basement) is framed with either 2x10 joists, engineered-lumber I-joists, glue-laminated beams ("glue-lams"), or flat floor trusses. Placing a wall on this floor structure may necessitate adding additional joists to transfer the load to the foundation and I-beam. Removing a wall reduces the loading on the floor but may affect how the roof is structured.

Ranch walls are typically composed of load-bearing exterior 2x4 wood studs. To allow large expanses of glazing, many "modern" Ranches use 4x4 timbers or wood-lam columns to provide support. Walls have gotten thicker to provide more R-value of insulation, and perimeter columns grow larger to support larger clear spans of glazing and doors.

Roofs can be framed with rafters but usually will employ machine trusses or, where exposed, wood-lams and structural decking. Clear-span trusses are common to the Ranch and may allow the removal of just about any internal first-floor wall below the truss as long as lateral bracing is maintained above and services are relocated.

Gable, hip, or "flat" roof

Stick built, trusses, or cedar wood deck on laminated beams

2x4 or 2x6 stud construction, or wood timber or lam columns

Floor structure of 2x joists or composite members that sit on steel beam and pipe columns

Concrete-block or poured foundation wall on concrete spread foundation

the house. If they do, you may be pleasantly surprised. If you live in or are buying a home designed by a local architect, he or she may be another source for the drawings. If the architect is no longer in practice, check to see if another architect took over the practice. Most architects will be happy to provide the drawings, and for a small reproduction fee, you can save time, money, and questions. If you cannot locate the firm, see if the public library has an architectural archive of local architects. Another source is the municipal office where building permits and plans are filed. If any permits were taken out for previous remodeling work, there may be an original or partial set of drawings on file or on microfilm. It also pays to check to see whether the original contractors are still in business (or their children may have taken over). Construction continuity is good too.

**Double sinks,** imported tile, elaborate woodwork, and custom pulls all add up quickly to a very expensive bathroom. With all the wonderful products on the market, it really pays to have a well-worked design before you shop for materials.

## WHAT ARE THE EXTREMES?

In chapter 1, we showed an example of a "gut rehab," which can be pretty extreme. At the other end of the spectrum is the remodeling of just one room. However, it's important not to underestimate the cost factor: "Just a bathroom" may mean all new plumbing, new fixtures, considerable electrical work, expensive finish materials, expensive demolition, and, depending on your location, a new septic system. Before you start any project, you need to do your homework. Visit showrooms, look at home improvement magazines, watch home improvement shows on TV. Don't pass up free seminars on financing offered by local lending institutions. You may find, depending upon the kind of living space you want, that gutting an existing house is actually more cost-effective than adding on or building new. Something as simple as removing one wall can make all the difference in the world.

### Historic House?

RANCH ROOTS

☆ **BELIEVE IT OR NOT,** that affordable 50-year-old Ranch in need of repair may come with an assistance package. If your home fits state and federal criteria for historic renovation, you may be eligible for tax credits, provided you follow the Secretary of the Interior's guidelines, which are available from your state historic society.

To qualify for a tax credit, you need to demonstrate that a historic event or person was associated with the home or, more likely, that the property has historic value through its cultural context or is 50 years old.

The Secretary of the Interior's guidelines describe helpful means and methods for maintaining your property. You are encouraged to retain as much of the original as possible; where replacement is necessary, the guidelines set standards that are appropriate to the original design and intent.

**Even though this house** looks as though it is a Bungalow or a Cottage, the overhead skylight is a tipoff that this was once a Ranch kitchen. The other clue is its rectangular shape and generous size.

## THE GOLDEN YEARS

As legislation currently stands, buildings 50 years old may be eligible for historic preservation status. You may be shaking your head thinking . . . how could a Ranch house be historically valuable? Remember, there are different categories of historic significance. In the case of the Ranch style, cultural as well as aesthetic importance is significant. It is more likely that an entire district will be recognized than an individual house. What does this mean to a homeowner? Unlike in Great Britain, where there are very strict historic preservation laws concerning both exterior and interior renovation, the United States uses financial incentives to encourage exterior renovation. No one is going to stop you from renovating your kitchen to suit your own taste. And while we can't image that a Ranch district designation will attract the tourist crowds that the Garden district

of New Orleans draws, we do think that help in preserving these neighborhoods for future generations of active families is both a sustainable and cultural investment.

Unlike Colonials and Capes with their center entry and Bungalows with their dominant roofs, Ranches are flexible and adaptable. While this gives you a lot of freedom, it also makes it more difficult to know when you've "got it right." You'll need to spend some time deciding what you want from your remodeling project, not just what is possible. If you are interested in respecting the integrity of the Ranch style, you must set limits. You'll have to decide whether the architecture, the furnishings, and the finishes should all work together to make a single statement. Even if you're a midcentury furniture collector, try to create a living house, not a museum.

# California Dreaming

ABOVE, **Curves in the countertop** and the glass shelves direct the eye to the new windows that incorporate the panoramic view of the backyard as an integral part of the new kitchen design.

FACING PAGE, **A quote from a 1958** *House Beautiful* magazine on Ranch houses sums up this renovation to a T: "Nothing anonymous about these rooms. . . they do not conform to any style of period, they reflect the wide-ranging interests and enthusiasms of their inhabitants. Old and new mixed together."

J UDY AND RON ARE BIG FANS OF JOSEPH EICHLER'S 1950s Ranch developments that highlighted Modernist design, open plans, and the seamless connection of interior and exterior living rooms. They were thrilled when they bought their 1965 Eichler custom-designed Ranch, tucked away on a cul-de-sac on Richardson Bay in Mill Valley, California. Their house was the last one built in the development, and it is smaller than many of the other homes in the neighborhood. Ron and Judy, like many Ranch owners, found the house perfectly suited to their needs, with one expensive exception—the kitchen.

## Easy as 1, 2, 3

Unlike the spacious open plan typified in the rest of the house, the 230-sq.-ft. kitchen was isolated from the other rooms by a white wood-paneled wall, most likely the legacy of a remodel by a previous owner. The east-facing kitchen had only one set of small slider windows, which didn't take advantage of either the view or daylight. The owners, who love to entertain, cook, and enjoy their garden view, knew the house could be improved if their architects understood how to update

an American classic. They hired the firm of Anna Scheidegger and Anthony Tobias, architects who are familiar with the residential work of Eichler and Frank Lloyd Wright. Their initial response was to follow in the footsteps of those two giants and open the space up as much as possible while making every foot of this small house functional.

The first step was pure logic. Remove the obscuring wall, and instantly the whole house is connected. Because this is a structural wall, two essential columns had to remain. The lowered ceiling of the kitchen helps to differentiate it spatially from the family room.

The second step was also logical: Add more and larger windows. The window over the sink was bumped out and is full height from countertop to ceiling. The extra depth and height of the new windows are enough to "dissolve" the wall and make the view part of the kitchen and family room. The sink window is still a slider, maintaining good natural ventilation. The second window is fixed, a picturesque feature.

And the third step was simple but brilliant: Choosing a limited palette of materials that reflect and bounce light while giving the illusion that the space is larger

ABOVE, **While the two columns** are necessary to support the roof structure, they're so well integrated into the design of the new breakfast bar that you forget about function. The single vertical support of the oval granite slab provides unfettered leg room.

RIGHT, **Although the previous** kitchen had plenty of storage and the cabinetry was in good condition, the room was isolated from the rest of the house, both functionally and in a design sense.

than it is. Glass, in the form of windows, cupboard faces, shelving, skylights, and exhaust hood, catches light, is see-through, and defies physical boundaries (an early hallmark of Ranch design). The existing all-white appliances were replaced with stainless steel, quite popular in the early '50s as well. The cool steel has a functional look and is highly reflective. Shadows and reflections in stainless steel give the perception of deeper space. The pale polished-granite countertops and the high-gloss floor tile continue the clean look of the original floor tile in the family room, tying the two rooms together.

To reinforce the visual connection but functionally separate the two rooms, the architects designed a kitchen island, which not only provides additional work space but also features a raised granite countertop that screens the cooking area from the adjoining room.

**The warmth of the maple-faced cabinets** is a perfect complement to the granite countertops and stainless-steel appliances.

## BEFORE AND AFTER

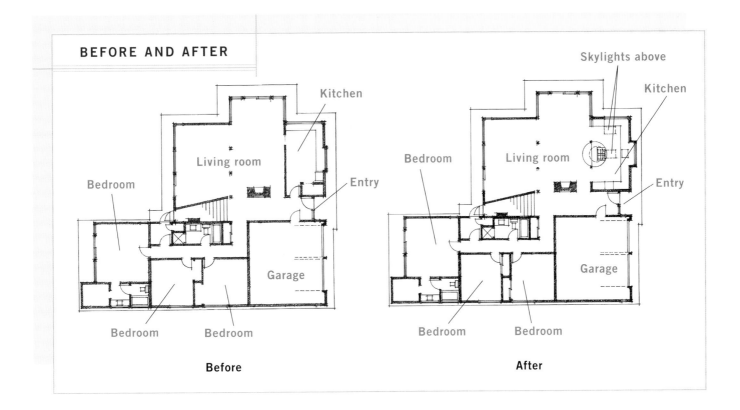

Before

After

FACING PAGE, **Built in storage** below the cooktop holds vases, napkins, and serving trays, all the things hosts need to get to quickly but may not want on display.

**The cooktop is set** into a generous curved granite slab that gives the cook just that extra bit of space needed for whisks, measuring cups, and spices in the heat of the moment.

## Practical Matters

Typical of California houses, the foundation is slab on grade. The utilities had to be threaded from the ceiling and boxed into the structural columns on either side of the island. A house with a basement can downdraft the ventilation through it, but a slab makes that impossible. The architects turned a potential problem into a design feature when they specified a ventilation hood that is as much sculpture as it is appliance.

## Updating Services

BECAUSE OF the threat of fire, insurance companies, municipalities, and banks may dictate electrical updates when a Ranch changes hands or home improvement begins. Most older residences have an inadequate electrical service for computers and built-in microwaves. The typical 60-amp 8-circuit panel should be upgraded to 100 (or even 200) amps with space for 22 or more circuits. Ground fault circuit interrupters (GFCIs) are required in bathrooms, kitchens, and utility rooms.

An additional bathroom, Jacuzzi, or second kitchen sink may stress your plumbing system. Before increasing water and waste lines, your plumber should check the municipally allowed capacity. If another water heater is needed, opt for one with an efficient recovery, which is quicker to refill.

Updating your heating system depends upon its type, capacity, and your needs. Air-conditioning is easy to add to an existing forced-air system. Fixing a drafty area may better be accomplished with an electric baseboard than expanding a costly hot-water or forced-air system. Major additions may require a separate, independent mechanical zone.

Updating the services in your Ranch is easier accomplished if you have a full basement; a slab-on grade can be a challenge. Depending on your needs, a licensed electrician, plumber, or mechanical subcontractor should be involved in this serious business.

# Two into One

FACING PAGE, **Sliding-glass doors** were commonplace in most Ranch homes, providing expansive views, light, and quick egress to the yard. Oddly, this house didn't originally have them. Adding a new set of doors is a relatively easy and inexpensive way to dramatically improve the daylighting and outdoor connection in your home.

H ALFWAY ACROSS THE COUNTRY IN MINNESOTA, another family owned a Ranch that posed the flip side of Ron and Judy's conditions. Wayne and Diane's custom 3,000-sq.-ft. home was twice the size of the average Ranch in their neighborhood, and they had not one but two small kitchens, both in one room. The previous owners kept kosher, and dietary laws require two separate sets of appliances, dishes, pots, pans, and cupboards. Wayne and Diane's family did not need the duplication; they wanted a more spacious eat-in kitchen.

## Planning Ahead

Wayne and Diane bought the home intending to remodel. But instead of jumping into the big projects right away, they opted to live in the house for a while and firm up their ideas. After eight years, they were confident that they knew what they wanted. Architect Robert Gerloff encouraged them to look beyond square footage and to consider materials, colors, and special details that would make the house their own. With three active, children (and pets), accessibility,

ABOVE, BELOW, AND RIGHT, **Vaguely Colonial,** with its "wrought-iron" hinges on the wood cupboards, boxed "beams," and "brick" floor, the existing kitchen (right) looked like thousands of Ranch kitchens. Some of the original cabinets were painted a soft gray-green and given translucent glass fronts, a total new look for a fraction of the price of new cabinetry.

**Noisy dishwashers have** been known to ruin the ambiance of a dinner party. Solid-core doors are more expensive than hollow-core doors, but when muffled sound is your goal, the money is well spent. The sliding doors can conceal the cook's chaos with a simple sweeping motion.

maintenance, soundproofing, and storage were all major considerations in the design. A huge bonus was that most of the changes could be made within the existing square footage, although the garage was bumped out for a mudroom to accommodate boots, coats, and kids' sports paraphernalia. The biggest projects were enlarging the kitchen and remodeling the two bathrooms.

## Colonial Revival

This Ranch, like many others, has elements of Colonial Revival detailing. Early Ranches followed on the heels of the ever-popular Colonial and Cape Cod–style homes, and contractors would hedge their bets when building the more modern Ranch style by including some familiar Colonial details. Wayne and Diane liked the balance of traditional and modern

**When the doors are open,** the whole color palette of the kitchen changes, and suddenly the room appears cooler and more expansive.

**Color is clearly the key** to the spirit of this kitchen, with deep purple, gray-green, and creamy white highlighting the warm woods of the cabinets and floors. The architect chose medium density fiberboard (MDF) for the island, finished with enamel paint for added protection against kicks and bangs.

design motifs and materials, and they decided to continue that look in the new kitchen. The decision to use traditional and readily available materials created a cushion in the budget for custom-design details. Formica for the working countertops, highly glazed square tiles of variegated hue for the sink wall, sliding-glass doors, and paint are all off-the-shelf materials; the alternating light and dark planks of Tasmanian oak for the floor, curly maple for the island countertop and the cupboards are special-order. The "command central" wall of built-in cupboards and desk, with a place for calendars, phone numbers, and permission slips, eases the stress of the hectic breakfast hour.

## BEFORE AND AFTER

Before

After

## Tiled and True

Both bathrooms needed to be updated, and a small
closet provided the perfect opportunity to create a first-
floor laundry room with much-needed built-in storage.
The children are all competitive swimmers, so the
underwater concept for their bath was a natural. The
blue-glass mosaic tile shimmers like a swimming
pool and is faithful to the use of mosaic tile made
of imported Venetian glass, in early Ranch home

**Lighting in bathrooms** can enhance the way you feel
about the way you look. Here, "yellow" fluorescent
lighting warms up a white bathroom and picks up on
the tawny browns of the ornamental band.

# Updating the Bath

**REMODELING A BATHROOM** allows you the opportunity to stamp your own personal style on your home while adding creature comforts.

The American Ranch was probably one of the first housing types to typically have two bathrooms. While the original master bath may not accommodate some of the newer and larger fixtures popular today, these original baths provide very good bones upon which to begin a basic update.

Plumbing fixtures may be outdated, the color range no longer desirable, or the plan inefficient. Maybe you're looking for additional or larger fixtures, better linen and towel storage, even some in-room exercise equipment. Fixtures and services probably haven't changed that much since your Ranch was built, so replacing them with new fixtures shouldn't prove too difficult. More contemporary Ranches will probably have thin-set tile, which allows for easier replacement. One thing to watch out for is updating a bathroom with a radiant-heated floor; any revision should be carefully worked out to avoid the concealed heat pipes.

Increasing space for new or larger fixtures can be a challenge. You might be able to borrow space from an adjacent closet or bedroom, or even cantilever 2 ft. to 3 ft. out into your yard. Large expansions of a walk-in closet, exercise room, and three-person whirlpool can best be accommodated by colonizing a spare bedroom. When expanding, try to use existing wet walls (walls with plumbing services already in them) and keep in mind that it may be more economical to add a new shower compartment or whirlpool than to renovate the whole space.

For now, a fun shower curtain and colorful pulls on the vanity give the bathroom a kid's look. With a quick change of the curtain and the hardware, the mood can be transformed from playful to sophisticated. The key is to pick permanent materials—tile and fixtures— that can be dressed up or down with inexpensive accessories.

bathrooms. The typical Ranch high-strip window affords both privacy and ventilation.

The parents' bathroom blends old and new and could be at home in a Bungalow. Translucent and transparent glass, mosaic tile and square marbled tile, chrome finishes, and fluorescent lights all add up to a 1920s look. But the zoning is completely contemporary. Each of the primary fixtures in the bath has its own space, so Debbie and Wayne can both prepare for the day without getting in each other's way. And if one wants to unwind with a long hot soak in the tub, the other can shower quickly and leave without having to wait for the bathroom to be available.

## Life's Little Chores

As every busy family with three kids knows, laundry is an ongoing chore. Considering how much time is spent doing the laundry, Diane wanted the room to be just as nice as any other room in the house (see the photo at right). With warm wood built-ins, good lighting, a handy folding counter, and convenient hanging space, even children can be enticed to do the laundry. The old excuse of being afraid of a dark and gloomy basement laundry room won't cut it in this family. Good design helps streamline daily life so that there is more time for the things everyone enjoys.

More storage wasn't the answer for this family. What they were looking for was useful and efficient storage that would help them put things away *and* find them when they needed them.

# Surprise Package

ABOVE, **As in the classic** Tiffany blue box, the gems of this simple Ranch are on the inside.

FACING PAGE, **The house improved** with deletion: The owners just kept removing walls until they got exactly the house they wanted.

M ARYLAND SUBURBS ARE FILLED WITH VARIATIONS of Roberta and Frank's 1969 red-brick one-story Ranch home. Like many Ranch buyers, they were shopping more for the right address than for the right house. They already knew that they would remodel whatever house they bought. What sold them on this particular house were the great neighborhood and the views from within the house to a beautiful park and golf course. They lived in the house for a few years before deciding on the final direction they wanted the remodeling to take. During the year it took to complete the remodeling, they set up housekeeping in the basement.

## Shuffling the Deck

At 2,000 sq. ft., additional square footage wasn't the problem. But because the house had so many small rooms and so much corridor space, it looked much smaller than it actually was. The rooms were not only small but the plan arrangement was awkward. The kitchen was a good distance from both the garage and the main entry. The living room and dining room were separated by a dark corridor. When Roberta and Frank interviewed Mark McInturff, they knew he was the

**From the minute** you step inside, the minimalist aesthetic of this Ranch remodel is delightfully clear. Rhythm, repetition, proportion, harmony, and tension are eloquently stated, while the landscape beyond is as beautifully framed by the double doors as any painting in a gallery.

right architect for the project. His initial reaction was that if they were willing to reduce the number of rooms, they could have a house that appeared much larger without adding on.

## House of Cards

Even though they bought a traditional-looking Ranch, Frank and Roberta's aesthetic is contemporary; they like clean, spare lines, and they wanted their new home to have the open feel of a loft space. This Ranch house was ideal for that approach. Only the exterior walls were bearing walls—none of the interior walls were structural. Any or all of them could fall like a house of cards, and the roof would remain in place. The first item for discussion was to define the "big idea" behind this remodeling. As much as possible, Roberta and Frank wanted to have a view to the park

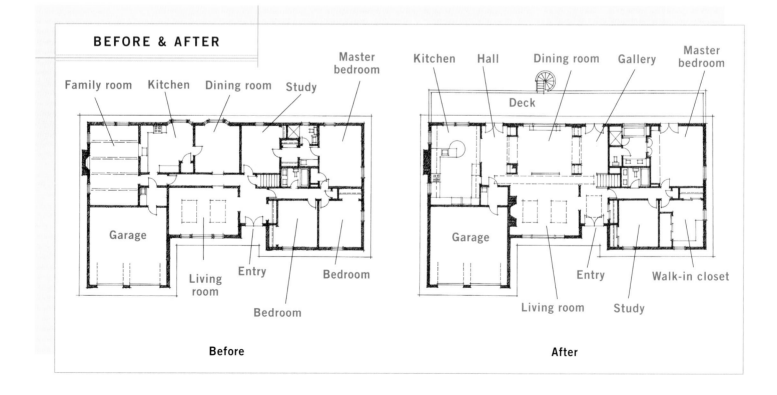

**BEFORE & AFTER**

Before — Family room, Kitchen, Dining room, Study, Master bedroom, Garage, Living room, Entry, Bedroom, Bedroom

After — Kitchen, Hall, Dining room, Gallery, Master bedroom, Deck, Garage, Entry, Living room, Study, Walk-in closet

**Before**

**After**

from every room. The obvious solution was to remove the dark and narrow corridor. Next on the list: What functions did Frank and Roberta want and where did they want them?

## Resale vs. Real You

For a resale, the owners knew they should keep all three bedrooms and the two full baths. The two smaller bedrooms and their bathroom did not warrant any major alterations; one is now a home office and the other a guest room. The master bedroom was just a tad too small, and the master bath was poorly laid out. So the walls came down to create a new layout that is both more gracious and more functional. The existing study was too small to be useful as a home office, but it was just right as a gallery space to display their glass and ceramics collection. With the wall removed between the

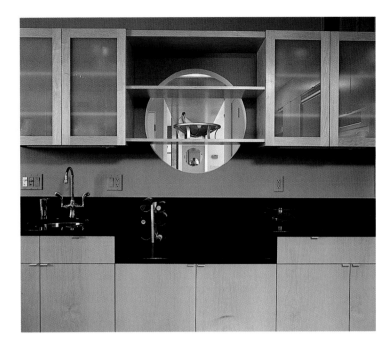

**A window over** the sink was traditional in Ranch kitchens. The architect cleverly placed a mirror behind the shelving over the wet bar, giving the host a "window" to the other rooms and providing the illusion of transparency in a solid wall.

## The Well-Shaped Room

**ARCHIMEDES USED IT,** Leonardo used it, architects use it today, and there's no reason why you can't use a proportioning system too.

Renaissance architects formalized a classical system based upon the ideal section of a triangle whose sides had a proportion of 1:1.618. This "golden section" was derived from "divine" human and natural measurements that could in turn be gracefully superimposed upon classic building elevations,

plans, and even rooms.

And it works. We use it every day in our office, whether for laying out a bedroom, evaluating a classroom, or designing a workspace. Admittedly we've rounded it off to 1:1.5 (easier to do the math in the field), which translates to a small bedroom of 10 ft. by 15 ft. The difference in dimension of unequal sides allows for a hierarchy of use or a focal point (square rooms, by contrast, are invariably ill-suited

to many functions). These proportions work especially well because the space is so much easier to lay out and to furnish. Most important, the resulting space inherently feels just right.

**Multitasking is something** we demand not only of ourselves, but of our homes. When closed, the fireplace surround appears to be a paneled wood wall; when open, it reveals an entertainment system. The owners have likened this built-in to a kimono, observing that every layer is beautiful and functional.

dining room and the study, the new gallery would be visible from the dining room. Most Realtors will tell you that a family room is a "must-have," but Frank and Roberta decided that they would benefit more from a larger dining room and a large kitchen than from an isolated family room. Down came more walls. Once the plan was finalized, McInturff joked that his major design tool was an eraser.

## Variations on a Theme

In the hands of some designers, a Ranch house without room separations could look more like a pole barn than a loft; it takes more than removing walls to make great space. McInturff tied the project together with three main elements: a limited palette of materials, color for variety, and a unifying element, in this case, an 80-ft.-long deck that runs the full length of the house, overlooking the park. Four sets of doors from different rooms all open out to the deck, respecting the Ranch hallmark that the flow from indoors to outdoors is seamless.

Sandblasted and translucent glass, warm maple, black slate, white pipe rail, and painted drywall make up the

**This remodeling was** for a house for two. The maple, slate, glass finishes, and display shelving are more sophisticated than you would find in a home revolving around the needs of small children.

**The frosted-glass sliding** panels allow the homeowners to change the dimensions of the room at will. For intimate dinner parties the panels close off the dining room from the living room. For large buffets, the panels can be moved to the side.

A common complaint about Ranch bedrooms is that they lack visual interest. Not this bedroom. The staggered ceiling heights, layered walls, and frosted-glass doors leading to the master bath create a sense of intimacy. And on the opposing walls, the large double clear-glass doors connect the sleeping quarters to the deck and to the rest of the house.

palette for the remodeling. In the public parts of the house you can see from one room into another; visual continuity is important. Maple was used throughout the rooms for the flooring, and it was carried up vertically into both the fireplace and the cabinetry. Even the refrigerator has a maple veneer, while the black slate on the kitchen countertops is the same material as the fireplace surround.

The architect suggested an interesting way to use color to create interest in large open spaces. As you face the kitchen, all the walls are painted with warm tones, yellow, charcoals, and red. When you turn to face the gallery, those walls are painted in cool tones, periwinkle, and cool white.

In the private zone of the house, the palette is more subdued. The master bedroom and bath have cool white and soothing aqua-tinted glass. Sandblasted glass in the bathroom door simultaneously provides diffused light and privacy. Books and the outdoor view provide the color for the master bedroom.

One of the goals of this project was for as many rooms as possible to have views of the park. That includes the bathroom. The interior window cut into the shower wall allows the bather to look out to the landscape beyond. The lower pane of glass is sandblasted, ensuring privacy.

# Santa Monica Peer

**The trellis visually** connects the exterior entry with the interior roof structure. This trellis is nicely detailed, with the special touch of the tapered beam adding lift and expression. When the vines grow up and over it, the entry will be a cool, leafy bower.

I N MANY PARTS OF THE COUNTRY, 875 sq. ft. of living space is small even for a condo. But if that 875 sq. ft. is in Santa Monica and only a mile from the Pacific Ocean, every square foot is pure gold. Otis's neighborhood dates back to the 1940s, the time when development pressure was just beginning to hit the Los Angeles area. Otis was attracted to this 1940s home because houses of that era tend to have "strong bones," the foundations were very well built, and they were built prior to any required earthquake codes.

## Good Things Come in Small Packages

Otis has renovated other houses of this vintage, and many of them share a similar layout. The rooms are small and space is wasted in useless corridors. You can move through the houses just fine, but there just isn't enough room to effectively lay out furniture so you can sit down and enjoy yourself. Otis's program for renovation was simple: one large room for entertaining, along with a bedroom and a guest room.

**In a few short growing seasons** and as the house's wood structure weathers to a soft gray, it will be difficult to separate it from the landscape, a true Ranch goal.

RIGHT, **Outdoor living made** the California Ranch the dream house of the 1950s. The view and easy access to the garden increases the living space of this small southern California Ranch home.

BELOW, **Aluminum sliding doors** would have been a more economical choice than these hefty wood doors. Saving a few dollars now is not worth the regrets for years to come. The doors are the focal point of the house from the garden and well worth the investment.

# A Simple Plan, Well Worked Out

Conventional wisdom tells us that entries make or break the way others perceive your home; great advice. In Otis's home, the front door opened directly into the living room, creating more useless circulation space. By simply relocating the front door and creating a trellised walkway, Otis transformed his bland Ranch into a house with personality—it now has an Address. This alteration achieved a couple of other good things in the interior. Otis created a foyer that lends a touch of formality to the arrival sequence, tempered by a little whimsy: He designed a window that acts as a message board. Friends who drop by can write a message, draw a picture, or leave a phone number on the window. Wax pencils are always available, as well as tissue to wipe off any mistakes. In addition, when the door was moved, the newly relocated bedroom gained an extra 8 ft., enough space to build a new closet in each of the bedrooms.

## Intimate or Private?

For a single person or a couple, intimately scaled spaces are far more desirable than private spaces. Doors seem somewhat irrelevant in an empty nest or for an individual's living space. Taking a clue from Ranch hallmarks, Otis zoned the house into public and private zones, and immediately the 875 sq. ft. appeared larger. By removing walls and doors, he created an open plan in a "Z" configuration. Now, sight lines rather than walls create intimately scaled rooms. The living room and the larger bedroom traded locations and suddenly all the quiet rooms were grouped together, and the active area was connected directly to the patio.

## Multitasking

At 12 ft. by 30 ft., Otis's living room is only slightly larger than an average ill-proportioned hotel room. To make the room feel spacious, he knew that the design

**This window-cum-message board** provides a whimsical touch at the entry and a measure of privacy for those inside. It is configured with two pieces of glass sandwiched with a white film.

### BEFORE & AFTER

Living room · Bedroom · Entry · Dining room · Kitchen · Entry · Bedroom

**Before**

Bedroom · Bedroom · Entry · Kitchen · Backyard · Dining island · Great room

**After**

RIGHT, **In a small space** every inch counts. The underside of this table is as well-thought out as the top. That's because the designer knew it would be visible when guests were seated in the living room. He even signed it, a sure sign of pride of ownership!

BELOW, **Setting tile in** a "crazy" pattern isn't as easy as it looks. But it is a project that, after some research, homeowners can do themselves for a one-of-a-kind shower.

would have to work with illusion rather than extra square footage. He gained height by removing the ceiling below the structure, which exposed the underside of the roof. He replaced the 2x6 ceiling joists with 4x6 rafter ties and introduced skylights. The only windows in the living room are square hopper windows directly under the roof structure; if they were any larger, there would be no wall space. The additional height and the increased natural light did wonders to change the perception of the room from a shoe box to a birdcage.

Otis likes to entertain. He knew that any conventional table seating six would eat up all of the available floor area. His solution was to design a table (it looks a lot like a surfboard) that could swing out from the counter when needed and swing back when he dined solo. The custom-designed combination dining and worktable also functions as a screen between the kitchen and living area.

## It Is All It's Cracked Up To Be

Abstract or geometric patterns formed with mosaic tile are one of the interesting features of Ranch bathrooms that many Ranch buyers today enjoy. Neutral colors

with very simple, (if any) patterning make a small bathroom look larger. Otis realized this tried-and-true rule wouldn't work in his house—his bathroom isn't small, it's tiny. He decided he might as well have some fun with it. He took a hammer to red and gray tiles and designed a "crazy"-patterned tiled shower wall that was sure to wake him up in the morning.

**A house is really** experienced in three dimensions. Removing the ceiling below the roof structure gave the room extra height

# Empty Nest

ABOVE, **Another surprise package.** The neo-Colonial exterior belies the contemporary interior but fits well into the neighborhood of Ranches.

FACING PAGE, **Removing walls** does not mean ending up with rooms without definition. Careful attention to texture and materials makes all the difference. All surfaces were considered: Expressed wood pegs call attention to the floor plane, an undulating window wall dispatches the cliché of a boxy Ranch, and the sculptural ceiling creates multiple lighting design options.

W HEN THEIR CHILDREN WERE AT HOME, Honey and Alan liked the fact that their house had a lot of "away" spaces. Once the kids were grown, Honey, a landscape designer, and Alan, an engineer, started looking at the house differently. What seemed cozy before now seemed disjointed. During the child-rearing years the house was always full of personality and life; now it seemed too quiet and inward looking. True to the old saying that cobbler's kids have no shoes, Honey realized her home did not have a great connection to the landscape, one thing every Ranch home is supposed to have. Most important, Alan and Honey had fun talking about what the two of them wanted their house to be; it was a great way to redefine their life as a couple.

Over the 28 years they had lived in the home, the children weren't the only things growing; the Georgia pines and the deciduous trees had also matured. What had started as a light-filled home was now so dark that it was almost depressing. Honey and Alan had three goals for their remodeling plans: to bring in more light, open up the floor plan, and improve the indoor-outdoor connections; all three are Ranch hallmarks.

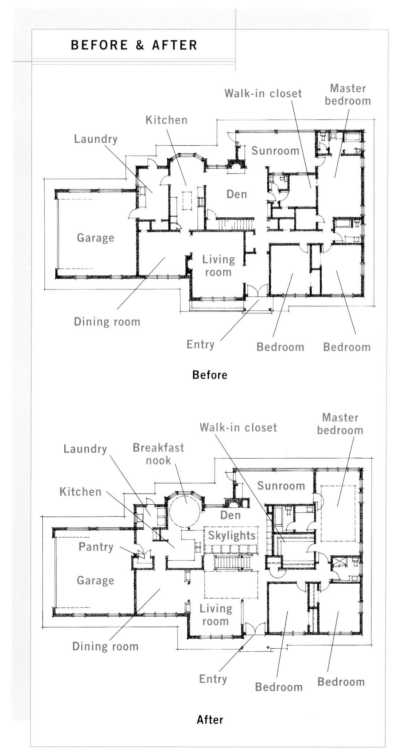

**Before**

**After**

Now that they knew what they wanted, they brought in August Architects to show them how it could be accomplished.

## The Daily Path

The architects, Karl and Vance, added one more Ranch hallmark to the list—clear separation of the public and private zones of the home. One big idea helped them organize all of the smaller ideas. They began by emphasizing the importance of a daily route from the master bedroom to the garage in the morning and the reverse at night. They suggested this path be distinctive in color and texture to accentuate its presence and to emphasize the newly instated cross-axial plan.

## Borrowing the Wright Way

As is typical in many midcentury Ranches, the stair to the basement was centrally located and near the entry foyer. This design feature enabled children to disappear into the rec room as quickly as possible. To Alan and Honey, the stair was a major obstacle, blocking the views of the landscape from the living room. Moving the location of the stair was not an option, but rethinking the design was. Removing the walls opened up the vista. A horizontal steel-plate banister now reinforces the feeling of movement along the main path, and the vertical steel pipe columns direct the eye to the layered ceiling. Frank Lloyd Wright's use of horizontal and vertical detailing is clearly understood by the two architects, and they used the principles to develop a fresh solution to Alan and Honey's particular problem.

**Skylights can appear** to be black holes at night. The lighting design for this house took that into account. Uplighting bounces off the coved ceiling and down spots reflect off the wood walls and variegated oak floor. At night, this room glimmers with honey tones.

LEFT, **Now that the** kids are grown, the house can take on a sophisticated look. The built-in wood cabinets wouldn't take the abuse of careening Tonka® Trucks but they are perfect for displaying (and concealing) collections. Mood lighting and an open plan combine to enhance entertainment opportunities.

FACING PAGE, **Connecting the indoors** with the outdoors was one of the major remodeling goals. The flooring pattern of this breakfast room recalls a stone patio, and the tall bay window offers a 180-degree view of the landscape beyond.

**The low soffit** over the kitchen work area brings task lighting closer to the work surfaces. Darker materials—wood, stainless steel, black countertops— help differentiate the functional kitchen from the relaxed living rooms.

## Ceiling Stories

Ceilings are vastly overlooked as a design opportunity. In this house, the ceilings could almost be called the fifth elevation: In every room they are an integral part of bringing in light and changing the perception of the spatial quality of the rooms. One of the common criticisms of Ranch bedrooms and hallways is that they lack the drama and detail found in the major living areas. Just raising the ceiling height in every room won't do the trick; it is contrast and function that make the difference appealing. Seated spaces enjoy lower ceilings that make the space seem cozier. If a lot of people are gathered to talk, a higher ceiling makes the space more formal, more special. Think about what kind of lighting you want. A chandelier needs height to show off to its best advantage, and small, high-intensity spots are more effective in a lower soffit.

ABOVE, **Walking on** the steel-and-wood detailed open staircase is a far different experience than that of moving through the typical Ranch "chute" to the lower level. To revolutionize your remodeling, try to think in terms of opportunity, not constraint.

RIGHT, **A monochromatic** palette can be boring. What adds pizzazz to this bedroom are the shadows cast by the indirect lighting in the ceiling cove and the spots on the elaborate molding of the window frames.

## Ceiling Remodel

**TAKING DOWN** a ceiling is a major commitment. Entire rooms will be uninhabitable for long periods, and drywall dust will be everywhere. If you are considering a complete ceiling remodel, we strongly suggest that you move out for the duration. As seen in the examples in the home shown here, however, the expense and inconvenience can be well worth it.

As an additional benefit, if you are considering upgrading your electrical system and want to implement a new lighting design, your options will be wide open if you are redoing your ceilings. And you won't have to worry about patching and painting.

## Clearing the Decks

While we are not yet empty nesters, we have begun to discover that as each "bird" leaves the nest an equal amount of clutter goes with them (or fills up the basement). The need for tabletops and counter space diminishes. You now have time to bring out and enjoy your collections, books, and music, and rearrange the furniture for adult comfort. The walls of Honey and Alan's home integrate built-in storage and display systems at every opportunity. This alleviates the need for a lot of furniture, and the walls are an ever-changing display of their personal interests. Custom lighting of these collections helps to set the mood and show off each object.

### HOME TO ROOST

When the kids come home for holidays, they are happy to find their childhood bedrooms intact. Alan and Honey took over a warren of small rooms that had been the sewing rooms—the original owner was a

professional seamstress—and converted them into a master bath and large walk-in closet. These rooms do not require natural light, and they provide the buffer between the private and public zones. When they relocated the bath from the far exterior wall, their bedroom gained a beautiful view of the landscape, and they achieved their goal of linking the indoors and outdoors.

**Color is a terrific** and inexpensive way to make a room seem larger or smaller, warmer or cooler. The deep orange of this room is warm, yet it provides a contrast to the light honey tones of the living room. The orange is picked up in the interior of the dining room display wall. A limited palette ties the open plan together. Too many colors would visually chop up the large space.

# CHAPTER THREE

# THE COMPLETE RANCH

ABOVE, **Many builder sunrooms** are tacked onto existing houses with no thought to the original house. From the brick foundation to the beefy sills and the slope of the roof, this glassy addition takes care to fit in and enhance the original house.

FACING PAGE, **One sure fire way** to update the look of an aging Ranch is to remove the carpeting that was so popular with Ranch builders. Gleaming wood floors provide a clean spare look that many new Ranch owners enjoy.

I F YOU ARE WONDERING WHETHER it is appropriate to add onto your Ranch, rest assured. It is not only appropriate, it is almost required as a Ranch hallmark. The mood of optimism during the postwar building boom was tempered by ingrained habits of thrift and caution. Ranch houses were designed to be built in stages, as the owners could afford to or when additional children necessitated more space. Many Ranch homes started out as simple rectangles and evolved into a veritable alphabet soup of options as an extra leg or two was added to form an "L" or an "H" shape. The famous Case Study Homes of the 1940s started small and were planned for expansion of the carport into a garage, a garage into a family room, and additional bedrooms. What many people today mistake for a Ranch that's too small may simply be one that didn't reach its full potential. Expansive is a Ranch adjective, either in its connection to the landscape, building additions, or entertainment opportunities.

**Bright, light, and private** are the motifs in this new bath. Skylights, mirrors, and interior and exterior glass-block windows ensure that this bathroom shimmers with both natural and artificial light. The gold accents add a little extra sparkle.

## The Building Boom Meets the Baby Boom

Builders, not architects, were the primary players in Ranch real estate. In 1948, costs of architect-designed homes ranged from $60,000 to $125,000—not exactly affordable for the average American family whose income hovered at around $4,000. By 1958, average income was close to $6,000, and builder Ranches, or "Contractor Contemporaries" as they were affectionately known, were down to $24,000 to $50,000. For the most part, single-family suburban living was still only an option for the upper middle class, who were leaving the cities for the suburbs in droves.

A new place to live meant new ways of living, and there was plenty of advertising available to instruct people on how to do it . . . in style. In 1958, lifestyle magazines were touting rooms for multiple uses to fit a family's changing moods. Kitchens were highlighted as the center of family life for both meals and entertaining. Two, even two-and-a-half baths, were no longer considered a luxury, but a necessity. The idea of a master bedroom with its own bath was beginning to catch on. And by 1970, 74 percent of all new construction was in the Ranch style. In less than 20 years, the 1,340-sq.-ft. Trade Secrets house (see p. 8) had grown to 2,150 sq. ft. and beyond. Additions were the name of the game.

Today, 2,000-sq.-ft. houses are considered small. Most people who buy small Ranches consider one of two options: Stay within the Ranch vocabulary and double the square footage, or, as you will see in chapter 4,

**Open the doors,** arrange the drinks and appetizers, and let the party begin. When the three sets of French doors swing open, the wall literally dissolves and the indoor and outdoor rooms flow together.

wrap the original Ranch in a completely different housing language and, at the very least, double the square footage.

### EXTENDED FAMILY

Not only were Ranch homes getting bigger, but the garages were expanding as well. Due to Detroit's inspired industrial designers, late-model cars were the ultimate status symbol. Trading in and up was common. Bigger and better garages were needed to accommodate that beloved family member: the car. In 1955, the basic garage was 20 ft. by 7 ft.; by 1970, it was 20 ft. by 20 ft. Not only did the garage house the two cars, but also the gas lawn mower, garden equipment, lawn furniture, and a tool wall or workbench. All the things that the urban dwellers of the 1940s had no use for had a special niche in the Ranch garage. Almost every suburban house in the late 1950s or early '60s had a stone or brick built-in barbecue pit or, at the very least, a patio for the redwood picnic table and the outdoor grill. Courtyard living, outdoor cooking, and in-ground swimming pools were the focus of suburban leisure time.

## Before You Add On

Even though we've given you carte blanche to add on, make sure you go about your addition plans slowly and deliberately. Just adding more square footage can complicate an already inadequate plan. New additions need

## The Future is Plastic

ranch style

**EVEN BEFORE** Benjamin Braddock was alerted to the benefits of plastic in the 1967 film *The Graduate*, plastic laminates were making a colorful contribution to the feel and especially the look of the Ranch interior. Plastic laminate was developed by Westinghouse Electric as an insulator for wiring but quickly found its way into home design. The postwar boom in Ranch construction created a huge demand for horizontal work surfaces, and plastic laminates were an inexpensive and durable way to deliver bright colors and bold designs.

Vertical applications of this material could be seen on accent wall panels, storage furniture, wall dividers, and doors.

Geometric patterns; 19th-century advertising art; primary colors; even some of the first faux prints of wood, stone, and bamboo were a part of the decorative Ranch kitchen, bathroom, or home office palette.

Ceramic, stone and conglomerate tiles, and even the more expensive slabs of solid plastic surfacing

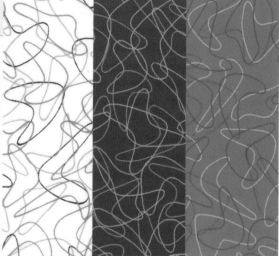

may have taken the place of plastic laminates in new kitchen or bathroom countertops, but plastic laminates still provide an economical and colorful accent with style for the Ranch interior.

to be integrated into the floor plan, the exterior elevation, and the site. Think very carefully about the house just as it is. Look at the houses in chapter 2 for suggestions about how to take an existing plan and alter it to work better for you. If you decide you need more space, continue analyzing the existing plan. In order to maximize the addition, the old plan may have to be reworked at the same time.

## MAKING THE REAL "IDEAL"

Much of our discussion is centered on the "ideal Ranch," but if you have been looking at Ranch houses to buy you know that many of them do not live up to the ideal. When you look at new properties or your present Ranch, think about the hallmarks of the style. Test the house against what it could become rather than what it is now. One reason why Ranches are a housing bargain is that people lack the ability to see creative solutions to surmountable problems. As you

**A small, quirky,** yet sympathetic decorative touch can personalize your house, giving it an address with a capital A. This beefy redwood column with the exposed hardware will eventually weather to gray, blending in with the siding of the house and the stone of the retaining wall.

## What to Do with the Garage?

**FROM ITS BEGINNINGS,** the Ranch garage has always accommodated a variety of functions beyond just housing the automobile—think garage bands and high-tech start-ups. Today, a typical two-car Ranch garage might be a candidate for conversion to a master bedroom suite, home office, or family room.

The garage (or carport) typically has a slab on grade foundation that sits on a grade beam or spread footings. A little investigative excavation may be needed to ensure that there's an adequate foundation; in the Midwest and Northeast that means a foundation carried below the frost line. Most attached garages have a 6-in. step below the first floor that acts as a carbon monoxide barrier. The change in elevation can be very helpful because it provides space to run electrical services and ductwork within the raised floor. This raised floor on sleepers provides insulation from the cold slab on grade. Because of their adjacent location, plumbing can usually be extended from the kitchen to the garage, by running services through your basement to the garage perimeter.

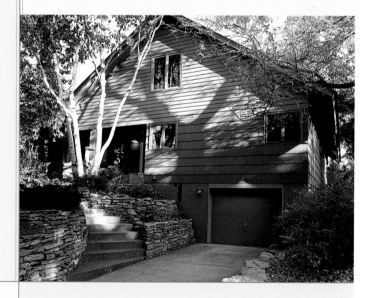

will see in the homes in this chapter, the Ranch is one of the most flexible housing styles to add on to.

A recent phenomena threatening Ranch neighborhoods is the teardown: Small Ranches built on great sites are often snapped up and torn down to make room for very large homes. Homeowners find that neighboring Ranches themselves aren't considered worth much, but the land beneath them is. While there isn't a lot you can do to stop development, you can recognize the value of what you have. If you already own a Ranch, adding on (even doubling the square footage) would more than likely be less expensive than building new. One way to figure out whether you should add on or buy a particular house is to ask yourself the following four questions:

✧ *Can you make strong indoor-outdoor connections?*
Although connectivity of indoor and outdoor spaces is a hallmark of Ranch style, this is one area where many Ranches disappoint. Look at each room and envision the possibilities for indoor-outdoor connections. Not all the connections have to be physical—views and light are as important as walking outside. Sit down in your favorite chair: Would you enjoy it more if you had a better view to the garden? Would you like to wake up in a lighter and brighter room? Would you use the backyard more often if the kitchen or family room were in a different location?

If the "outdoor living room" is little more than a large and undefined lawn, think of the large lot as a blank canvas upon which you can create a yard that is uniquely suited to your lifestyle. Consider who will use the yard. Adults, teenagers, small children, and pets all have different design requirements. But instead of designing four separate landscapes, all the requirements can be blended into one seamless design.

✧ *Can the entry become an "Address"?* A good entry is an important Ranch hallmark, but many of the Ranch builders of the '60s and '70s forgot to include it. This is one design feature that is relatively easy to reinstate, and it can set the tone for the way you (and your guests) feel about your home. Good Ranch entries remember that casual does not mean intimate. Greeting guests in a foyer is much more pleasant than having the front door open directly into the living room.

**The low-voltage** pendant lights hung over the buffet counter resemble fine restaurant lighting. Task lighting under the cabinets is softer and more direct than the eerie fluorescent lights of the 1960s Ranch.

**The deep soaking** whirlpool tub (complete with built-in grab bars) is surrounded by tile set in a bold pattern. The scale of the room is intimate but not confined. A deep-set skylight provides the necessary headroom as well as natural light.

✧ *Can the flow of spaces be improved?* As you'll see later in this chapter, some of the changes the home-owners made are dramatic. It may seem extreme to swap kitchen and living room locations, and conventional wisdom tells us that there is considerable expense involved in moving any "wet" room (one that has plumbing). But if you are so uncomfortable in your own house that you are contemplating moving, then that is reason enough to justify a major reworking of the plan, especially if you are considering adding on. Deciding where you need additional square footage is more important than just calculating how much square footage you think you need.

✧ *What amenities does your present home lack?* This is one decision that only you and your family can make. Ask family members to describe their dream house. Then ask them to rank their listing, from "pie in the sky" to "must-have." Daydreaming and implementing are two different realities. While you may enjoy a fire-place in a bathroom in a resort setting, it's probably a design feature you can do without in your own home. You don't have to be entirely practical—hand-set tiles are one luxury almost everyone can afford.

This chapter shows five homes that have been added onto within the Ranch hallmarks. Almost every kind of option is shown—one added up, one converted the garage into a master suite, and each one dramatically changed its look and improved the livability of the house.

☆ # Ranch Windows

**ONE OF THE HALLMARKS** of Ranch style is the integration of large planes of glazing to enhance the open plan and bring the outdoors in. Ranch houses accommodate a variety of window types, from the picture window to the awning and casement, often in joint assemblies. While the double hung is seldom used, it sometimes appears as a horizontal slider. Sliding patio or swinging French doors also fit the Ranch vocabulary. Colonial Ranches may include a bow or bay window. A new window type is the European-inspired tilt turn that allows full opening but also tilts out for efficient ventilation on sides and top.

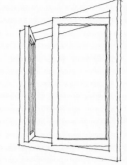

Casement (double acting)

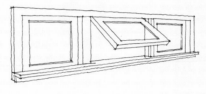

Tilt turn

Awning or hopper

Bay window

Glider or horizontal slider

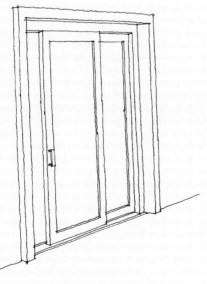

Sliding French door

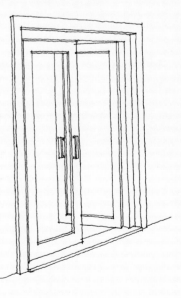

Jalousie window

Swinging French door

# Courtyard Living

The indoor-outdoor connection in a Ranch begins at the front door, and in this house it continues all the way out to the backyard.

BARBARA AND ROB'S STORY is one we've heard many times before, and for that very reason, it's worth repeating. Less than a year after moving into their home they knew they would either have to move or add on. Their 1950s-vintage California Ranch home was quaint and in a great location, but since it was 1,650 sq. ft. and had only two bedrooms, the family of four found it was just too small. When they started looking at other homes they quickly realized that every one they saw, regardless of size, needed remodeling. They went house and looked at their own home in a different way.

Rob, a landscape designer, saw great potential for a courtyard addition that would take advantage of long views from the house into the narrow, deep yard and tie the pool to the house. They hired architect Jeffrey Tohl to help them revitalize their aging, drab house into a spacious contemporary home that celebrated indoor-outdoor living. Previously, the couple had lived in a Mediterranean climate and enjoyed high ceilings, natural light, and bright colors. They wanted to incorporate those elements into their California home.

**A lot of Cliff May,** a little stage set, and a pair of committed homeowners rescued a too-small Ranch from possibly becoming a teardown. The architect borrowed from local building materials—stucco and metal siding—and the Spanish patio concept to create a contemporary Ranch.

**The cutouts in the walls** and ceilings give the rooms an added dimension of depth. Each room offers a visual invitation to another room. The use of color draws attention to the fireplace and enhances the unfolding of the wall planes, which resemble structural origami.

# Cosmetic Surgery

One advantage of living in the house for a year was that the family recognized that the organization of the floor plan of the original house worked just fine for them. The problem was that the rooms felt cramped. Several things contributed to that feeling. The windows were tiny, the walls were paneled with pine that had darkened over the years, and the fireplaces were dark brick. The dark colors and heavy textures made the rooms look and feel smaller than they actually were. The landscape resembled a jungle, smothering the house and blocking daylight. After careful consideration, the couple realized that most of the problems were cosmetic, not structural—simple alterations could transform the original house.

**It's easy to go overboard** with kitchen design. This kitchen expresses the family's priorities. They opted for storage below the work surfaces, tucked out of sight from the major living space, rather than additional hung cabinets.

## BEFORE AND AFTER

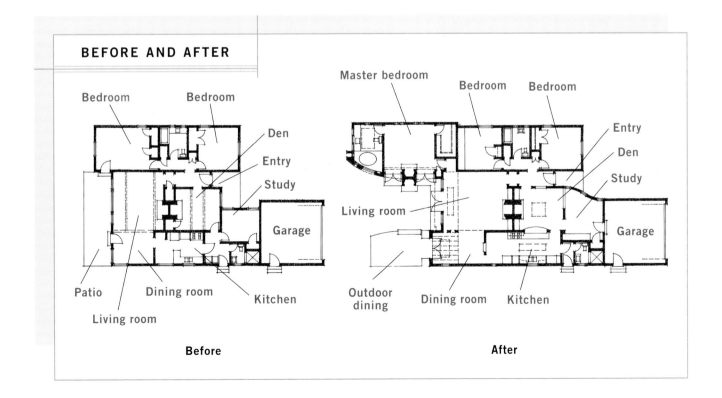

Before

After

**The wall cutouts** are carefully considered to do two things. As you walk through the house, they allow the rooms to open up to one another. But when you are seated, the half-walls of the den provide an intimate enclosure, focusing on the hearth that warms the body and the books that warm the soul.

**The ceiling in** the master bedroom is 6 ft. taller than any of the other ceilings in the home, distinguishing this private room from the rest of the house. Tall, narrow, deep windows give the room a garret-like atmosphere, even though it is on the ground floor.

## Baby Steps

When you compare the Before and After plans on p. 89 you can see that the changes made to the original floor plan were minor. Luckily for the budget, the existing bathrooms and kitchen just needed updating, with no major relocation of plumbing or other services.

Most of the original load-bearing structure remained intact, and only a few walls were reconfigured for better visibility or access. From the exterior, the roof retained its one-story profile. On the interior, the ceilings were removed to expose the structure, creating visual interest and an additional 2 ft. of height. Skylights added to the den and the kitchen brought light into the center of the home. The new color palette of yellow, white, terra-cotta, and black, combined with the smooth, sleek textures of plaster, drywall, wood, and stone, makes the rooms appear larger than they actually are.

## A Warm and Welcoming Home

The existing home had back-to-back brick fireplaces in the den and the living room. In the addition, Rob and Barbara liked the idea of connecting two separate rooms with a special feature, the double-sided fireplace that is the focal point of the new master suite. The

**The den is an interior room,** with no direct views outdoors. Shared glass panels, light sources, and fireplaces between the living room (shown here) and the den connect the room with the rest of the house.

# Fireplace Options

**AS IN ALL AMERICAN** housing types, the fireplace in a Ranch is a visual and social focal point. Considering the modesty of the Ranch form, there's a surprisingly rich variety of options.

The typical Ranch contemporary fireplace has a simple mantel that extends horizontally to house log storage and entertainment center, while 78 records are replaced by DVDs in the built-in bookshelves above. Fireplace options expanded with the popularity of the Ranch, embracing see-through or corner fireplaces in partial walls that served as room dividers as well as storage walls. Steel fireplaces hung from the structure above and provided uninterrupted views from sunken living room pits. Scandinavian wood-burning stoves were an attractive freestanding option.

Today, all of these options and more are available. The construction of a masonry fireplace is a high art, and if it already works well, confine your changes to cosmetics. New finish materials can be laminated to existing surfaces. Conversion to gas is an energy and operational consideration for some fireplaces.

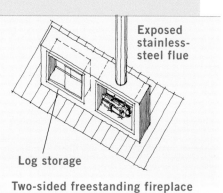

Exposed stainless-steel flue

Log storage

**Two-sided freestanding fireplace**

Hearth extends to bench or log storage

**Corner fireplace (open two sides)**

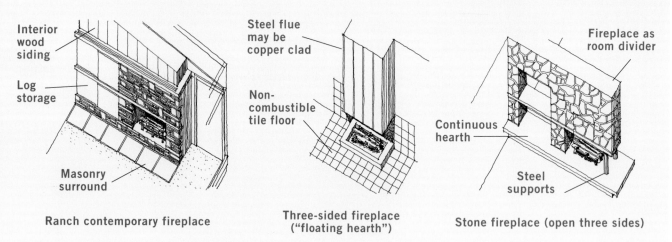

Interior wood siding

Log storage

Masonry surround

**Ranch contemporary fireplace**

Steel flue may be copper clad

Non-combustible tile floor

**Three-sided fireplace ("floating hearth")**

Continuous hearth

Steel supports

Fireplace as room divider

**Stone fireplace (open three sides)**

other hearth faces the patio, which is accessed from the bedroom through two sets of French doors. The bedroom suite gives the parents a private refuge, but they are still closely connected to the family-centered courtyard.

The indoor-outdoor connection is also acknowledged in the master bath. A glass-block wall behind the deep tub ensures privacy and light, and the vertical clear windows give glimpses of the pool and the landscaped berm. Horizontal slider windows, so typical in Ranch houses, provide ventilation and a distant view of the eastern sky.

LEFT, **In a one-story house**, you can run plumbing through the ceiling, which frees up the exterior walls for windows. The shower head floats above the middle of the tub, allowing the user to shower "in the round."

BELOW, **Many patios are** just the space outside the back door; not so with this patio. The same careful attention that was paid to the interior rooms was paid to this outdoor room. Changes in level, variety in colors and textures, depth of the wall, and height of the "ceiling" were all taken into account.

## The Western Ranch

Ranch pioneer Cliff May (see p. 15–17) would doubtless have approved of this project. It fulfills his idea that families should build for the way they really live— relaxed, secluded, and comfortable. The 625-sq.-ft. built addition to the original house is only part of the story. May always said the patio was the key feature of the Ranch house. In the southern California climate, a patio can be a true year-round outdoor room.

Rob and Barbara's courtyard concept is successful because they carefully considered what would make the courtyard livable. First, ease of access. There are multiple entries into the courtyard: two entries from the master bedroom suite, double doors from the living room, and double doors to the dining room. Second, privacy. No one feels comfortable dining, swimming, and entertaining in full view of the neighbors. The lot is walled and landscaped to screen the family from the neighbors. The patio is embraced by the exterior walls of the addition. These walls provide shade and protection from the sun and wind and help to spatially define the patio as a room. A total of 440 sq. ft. of additional flexible outdoor living space is gained with the grass-and-paved patio and the paved outdoor dining room.

# Ranch
# with a Mission

**Even if you double** the square footage with your addition, it doesn't have to be obvious from the street. To make this addition fit in as closely as possible, it was stepped back from the original house, and the low terrace wall was continued. After all, one reason the homeowners bought this house was that they liked the way it looked!

W ITH ITS STUCCO WALLS, large windows, and tiled roof, this 1928 Denver Mission-style Ranch is about as close to the original adobe Western Ranch as you can get. The original one-story 900-sq.-ft. home was once home to a family of six. When David and Gay were shopping for a house, they were attracted to the thoughtful and charming details of this diminutive home, inside and out. Each window was slightly different from the others (but perfectly suited to its own room), and French doors opened out to the patio and outdoor fireplace. A low-walled patio led to the front entry, reinforcing the Mission style. David owns a construction company, so the idea of a major addition was not daunting. Collaborating with a local architect, Jim Mitchell, David designed a new family room, kitchen, and master bedroom suite, adding 800 sq. ft. to the home.

## Finishing School

The house was a true diamond in the rough—all the rooms needed updating. David and Gay planned the addition so that it would reinforce the Western patio style, which meant that instead of adding up or just to

**The difference between** simple and plain is a question of detailing. A plain room has very little character; it lacks a sense of design intent. A simple room is one in which all the details work together to express one clear idea. The windows are set deep into the walls, and the frames are made up of complex pieces, adding ornament and interest.

**The backyard is divided** into public, semipublic, and private zones, just like the interior of a Ranch home. The clay-tiled courtyard, slightly higher than the other outdoor spaces, is well located for entertaining. The bedroom has its own paved seating space, screened by the large patio's plantings.

**The homeownwers were charmed** by the look of this little house. One of their updating goals was to double the square footage, without halving its charm.

one side, the addition would be built as wings on either side of the rear of the original house. The new kitchen and family room were built to the south and the master bedroom suite to the north, with an indoor corridor and outdoor patios that marry the two additions.

The courtyard faces south and east. Early morning light filters into the master bedroom suite through the high windows. The patio connected to the family wing is bathed in southern light, perfect for late dinners in the summer or for capturing the last glimpse of the winter sun. A strong sense of enclosure is created by the story-and-a-half height of the additions.

## The Big Idea

Every successful project has one big idea behind it, in concert with the 100 small decisions that pull the whole thing together. For Gay and David, it was the arches,

Not many bedrooms are designed from the vantage point of someone lying in bed. In this bedroom, most of the visual interest is at ceiling level. Recessed can lighting washes the ceiling with light at its highest point, while the clerestory windows allow for star-and-moon gazing after the lights are turned off.

which reinforce the idea that openings in a wall can look and feel as though they are part of the structure. The new windows and doors are the major design element in the remodeling. The couple decided that they would pay a good deal of attention to the framing around the windows and doors to emphasize the thickness of the walls. The existing wall construction was 8 in. of full masonry, which resulted in the typical 4-in. depth of a window being inset 4 in. from the exterior face wall. From the exterior, the windows look as though they have been "punched" into the wall. The new construction was built the same way—not the most

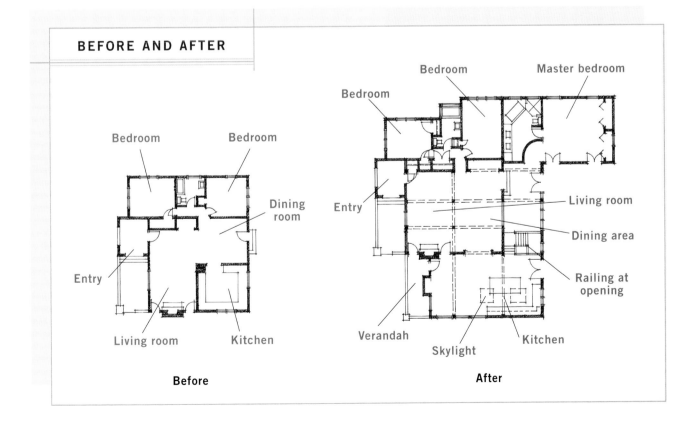

## BEFORE AND AFTER

Before

After

FACING PAGE, **The tall ceilings** and exposed structure give the room a sense of drama and formality beyond what most people associate with Ranch homes. A blazing fire sets a welcoming tone as the family and their guests sit down for dinner.

ABOVE, **Light, open, and airy** does not necessarily mean contemporary. The dark cherry cabinets with wrought-iron pulls combine with the random chisel finish of the limestone backsplash to give the kitchen a traditional handcrafted Mission look.

ABOVE RIGHT, **The homeowners intentionally** distressed the paint on the kitchen island to add texture. The orange underpainting glows beneath the crackled slate-green overcoat, picking up the warm tones in the limestone countertop and the oak floors.

economical method, but it does provide good thermal insulation and sound isolation from exterior noise.

## Major and Minor Chords

Gay and David both liked the idea of integrating exposed timber columns, beams, and trusses as part of the interior design. They ripped out the existing ceiling and took the new ceilings up to a 12-ft. height; new pine collar beams and columns support the structure. Because the structure is exposed, David decided that mortise-and-tenon construction, a nod to the Arts and Crafts movement, was the appropriate look. The tall ceilings in the dining room, combined with skylights in

LEFT, **Limited in space** but not in spirit, this shower has it all. The tilework is reminiscent of the brickwork on the exterior, while the skylight brings in the morning light. The deep sill and walls eliminate the need for a shower door or curtain, and the built-in bench is an amenity most people would enjoy.

FACING PAGE, **Two steps down** from the dining room, the informal breakfast room off the patio doubles as a foyer to the master bedroom suite. The two high square windows bring light deep into the dining room.

## Using Salvaged or Recycled Materials

**WHETHER YOU'RE RESCUING** a 1960s Ranch or building new, you might want to think about integrating salvaged or recycled building materials into the structure. This approach can deliver quality materials, historic finishes, and craftsmanship detail, while representing a socially relevant and environmentally appropriate reuse of readily available building materials. It may also be an economical way to add charm and distinction to your home.

• Consider a recycled brick accent at the entry or fireplace, and recycled pavers on the patio.

Stone veneer can be reborn as countertop, hearth paving, or wall base. Take care to trace the history and appropriateness of your salvage. A landscape architect friend of ours built a fireplace surround of recycled marble. It wasn't until the heat of the first fire that he discovered the stone had been a toilet partition!

• Old wood floors, trim, and paneling are widely available. Reused timber structures and roof decking may provide the bones for a major addition that plays to the rustic appeal of the original Ranch house.

• Antique electrical fixtures need to be updated to current standards before inclusion. Plumbing fixtures should be evaluated with professional installers on a case-by-case basis. That nostalgic undercounter sink so popular today just might be easier to purchase (and install) as new.

Another word of caution: The Ranch was the first housing type to take full advantage of uniform sizing of building components, and windows and doors are better updated with new, more energy-efficient replacements rather than recycled units.

the kitchen and the two bathrooms, enhance the light, airy, and open feel that the homeowners wanted.

Interior finishes are kept to a simple palette that showcases the differences in detailing without over-whelming them. All interior trim is vertical-grain fir, with a clear natural finish to highlight the variations in the color and grain of the wood. Most of the new floors are 2-in. select oak to match the existing floors, except for the master bedroom, where Gay and David chose salvaged long-leaf yellow pine for the floors for a different look from the more public rooms.

In keeping with the Mission style, one-of-a-kind tilework was used in the two bathrooms. The kitchen has a large island that is part breakfast table, part work space, and part storage cabinet. The top is a thick slab of Italian limestone with a simple honed finish. The same stone is used for the kitchen counters.

# Refined and Simplified

ABOVE, **The glassy addition** replaces a 150-sq.-ft. screened-in porch. The new addition, which adds 510 sq. ft. of four-season living space, brings in more light and provides more relief from the weather than the porch ever did. Special care was taken during construction not to damage the mature maple tree.

FACING PAGE, **Instead of yelling** at the kids to get their feet off the furniture and sit still, the parents in this family encourage their children to grab a book, put their feet up, and swing the afternoon away.

THE ORIGINAL PLAN FOR THIS ADDITION was ambitious. It included three exterior patios, an open family room, a piano alcove, a utility room connected by a breezeway to the husband's home office and workshop, and an office for the wife closely connected to a classroom for their five home-schooled children. At first, the homeowners were very excited about the project, but as they studied the plans it dawned on them that the addition would overwhelm the scale of their 1960s 2,800-sq.-ft. Ranch and require the removal of several mature trees.

If you have plans for a large addition, it pays to look around your neighborhood first. If the addition will make your house the largest on the block, you might want to reconsider. For one thing, if everyone built a large addition, the neighborhood character would change dramatically. For another, common-sense real estate advice dictates that you shouldn't buy or own the biggest house on the block.

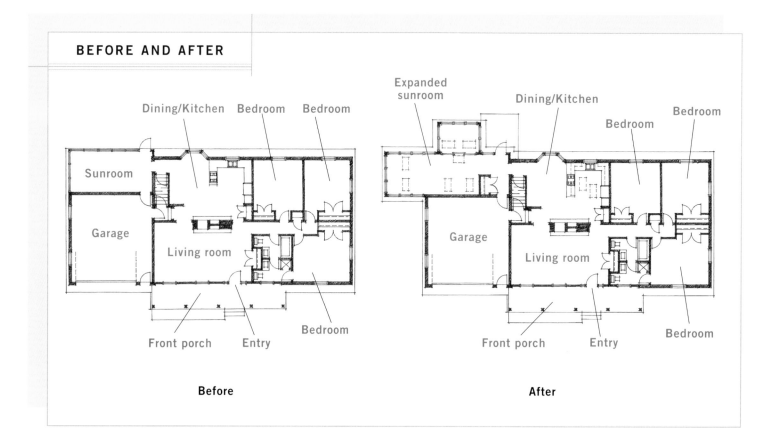

**Before**

**After**

## Round Two

The homeowners went back to their architects, Pam Harwood and Bill Tabberson. In the next round of discussions, they reconsidered what, in addition to square footage, was important to the family. What they really wanted was a light, bright, multifunctional family space, close to the kitchen and the garage, and one that allowed them to keep the large trees in the yard. At just over 500 sq. ft., the built addition is only a third of the square footage of the first proposal. The family of seven finds that it meets their day-to-day needs perfectly, and on special occasions such as birthdays and holidays it can accommodate a crowd. And there's always the option of a second addition should the family need more room in the future.

## One-Room Schoolhouse

This home is in the upper Midwest, an area rich in the history of one-room schoolhouses, which also served as civic meeting houses and places for community celebrations. Those functions pretty much summed up what the family needed. The fact that the children are home-schooled posed some interesting challenges. Indiana has its share of severe winter weather, and "cabin fever" is a real condition. The addition needed to be warm and inviting even in the winter months. Fortunately, due to improved technology, the addition resembles a green-

**A rectangle is** the most flexible shape to work with if you want to be able to subdivide the room into several activity areas. And when you host family celebrations or a pasta dinner for your kid's swim team, rectangular rooms allow you to link several long tables together and still have room to move around.

house more than a schoolhouse; so there's no need for a potbellied stove heat source today.

Summers in Indiana can be hot and humid, so ventilation is an important consideration in a "greenhouse." The lower hopper windows are all operable, allowing fresh breezes to waft through the room. Electrically controlled blinds permit shading of the skylights, which are cut into the deep ceiling facing east, west, north, and south. This glass pavilion provides a panoramic 180-degree view of the yard, and the light in the sunny room is bounced and filtered by the white surround of the skylight, which bathes the space in a soft glow. To ensure that the room is inviting at night, the recessed can and track

**Natural ventilation** is provided by opening the lower hopper windows, and the room is heated and air conditioned with forced air. The hammock room in the small projecting bay can be closed off from the larger space.

## ☆ Ranch Storage

**COMING FAST** on the heels of booming American consumerism, the Ranch provides more storage space than any other previous housing type.

Designers George Nelson, Charles Ray Eames, Hugh Acton, and many others developed freestanding storage units that did double duty as open room dividers, or updated the Bungalow hutch. Space-age laminates and bright colors were employed, along with light natural woods. High design and industrialization were applied

to make Ranch life more comfortable and better organized. Adjoining bedrooms enjoyed "zigzag" closets and sound insulation. Garages were bumped out at the rear to provide for labor-saving garden equipment. And everything that couldn't fit anywhere else and used to go into the attic went into the Midwestern Ranch basement.

Today the thirst for consumption continues, and even more storage is required. Realtors list the walk-in closet

(WIC) at the top of the checklist in a new house purchase. Additional room for Ranch storage can be achieved by turning two small bedrooms into a master bedroom/bath with adjacent WIC. Most new construction will incorporate this same combination. More economical closet bump-outs up to 2 ft. deep can be cantilevered off perimeter walls without the need for a foundation. And for those Midwestern Ranch owners . . . they'll always have the basement.

fixtures are positioned to wash the white walls with light, crisscrossing each other to fill the entire room with bounced light and avoid large areas of deep shadow.

Even in close families, everyone needs an "away" space. The south-facing room can be closed off from the large room for quiet reading, playing an instrument, or daydreaming in the hammocks. With a view to the large yard on three sides, it feels as though you are miles from anyone else. The naturally finished wood contrasts with the white-painted interior of the larger room.

## Everything in its Place

Five active children, with their own separate interests, present an interesting design problem. How can they stow their athletic equipment, musical instruments, books, and school supplies and be able to readily retrieve them? The architects came up with an efficient system that is also attractive—no mean feat! They designed a storage wall in the mudroom that connects the garage to the house. Based on the module of a laundry basket, the storage system provides space low to the ground that's convenient for teaching even a toddler to clean up. The system is deep enough to stow off-season items in the back and in-season items in the front. And it is strong enough to protect violas and violins.

**Modular construction** and preassembled parts were used in early Ranch construction to keep costs down. This modular storage system is flexible and adaptable to growing children—each unit can be easily and quickly personalized for the height and habits of each child.

# Back to the Ranch

ABOVE, **The same palette** of materials and colors is used indoors and out, reinforcing the home-owner's understanding that the term *outdoor room* is more than an expression, it is garden architecture.

FACING PAGE, **This combination kitchen** and family room offers some helpful hints for those who enjoy entertaining. The three informal seating areas are easy to enter and leave, which encourages mingling. There are plenty of surfaces for drinks and plates. And the centrally located double French doors offer a clear invitation to the patio.

L IKE MANY HOUSE HUNTERS, Herb and Pat fully anticipated that if they bought a Ranch it would need full-blown remodeling. This 1,500-sq.-ft. remodeled tract Ranch is in a great location on a secluded canyon road, yet is close to shopping and only a short commute to the freeways. The hills behind the home are too steep to be developed, and the mature landscape screens each house from its neighbor, but the homes are close enough together that the street has a neighborly feel. Pat and Herb were very excited about the remodeling potentials that awaited them.

## Missed Opportunities

The house is just a stone's throw from many of the icons of modern residential architecture built in the 1940s, but the original builders must not have looked out their car window on the way to the site. They turned their back on every positive aspect of the site and of good modern design.

The garage blocked the best view, and the plan was a warren of small rooms with limited visual or physical connection to the outdoors. The woodwork was dark, the windows small, and the glare made it difficult to see inside or out. Pat, an interior designer who had worked

# Opening the Windows

**IT'S A NATURAL** inclination to want to get more light into any home, but there are several things to bear in mind before you start ripping open a wall for a larger window or door. First, consider how any new or expanded openings will fit with the other proposed changes—think about the view, privacy, circulation, function, connection to the outdoors, daylight, and aesthetics. Increasing the level of daylighting is a commendable goal, but there can be too much of a good thing. Adding windows to a western exposure without the benefit of a significant view can bring in summer heat and year-round afternoon glare.

When you cut holes in exterior walls, structural concerns become paramount; you'll need to consult an architect or engineer. Most Ranch doors and windows are framed with overhead beams called lintels made of steel angles, channels, or occasionally wood "headers," like 2x10s which support the overhead weight. For proper bearing, these lintels should project 8 in. beyond the opening on each side. Openings require framing above as well as on the sides to carry the weight to the foundation wall.

Dropping the window sill depth is less of a problem because the installed header is already holding up its end. Consolidating a line of picture windows or terrace doors into one expansive, uninterrupted opening may require replacing the smaller headers and the columns between them with one continuous, deeper structural member overhead and columns on the sides.

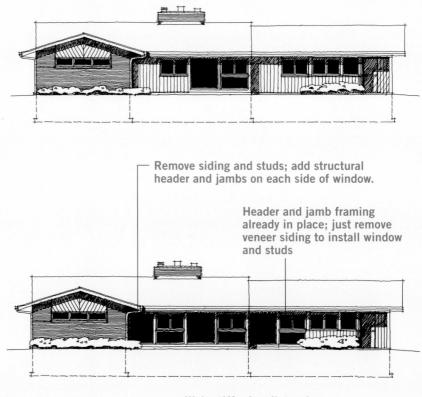

Remove siding and studs; add structural header and jambs on each side of window.

Header and jamb framing already in place; just remove veneer siding to install window and studs

Web stiffening (lateral bracing) may be needed.

with architectural firms, could see that the house had possibilities. In fact, she envisioned a reworked plan that would make it even more of a Ranch than it had been. Herb and Pat brought in architects Ann Agnew and Don Boss to help them realize their vision.

## Back to Basics: House and Patio

Pat and Herb liked the bones of the house, and they wanted to keep the low profile of the single-story Ranch, appreciating that the style was compatible with the neighborhood and the setting. To stay on track they kept their goals basic: to fill the entire house with natural light and create a setting for seamless indoor-outdoor entertaining.

The house was built with just two bedrooms, which was fine with Pat and Herb, but they did want the master suite to be private, set apart from the main house. An outdoor living room would be the interlocking keystone of the remodeling, visible and accessible from all the major living spaces. The sense of outdoor rooms, or garden architecture, is now reinforced by the use of

ABOVE, **With the rest** of the house so open and public, it's necessary to have an intimate place designed specifically for concentration. The desk faces a blank wall, while the windows provide daylight but not distraction.

LEFT, **Only the roofline** of this Ranch is original: Every room has been rearranged, renovated, and redirected to the private patio in the back. Even the carport is new. The remodeling holds onto the Ranch hallmark of presenting a blank face to the street.

**Fireplace in the bedroom?** When the fog rolls in off the ocean, a fire in the fireplace is just the thing to take the chill out of the air. The textured black stone fireplace surround is a nice counterpoint to the abundant smooth, sleek white surfaces.

**While transparency was an** important design concept in opening up this once dark and cramped house, very few people want to feel as though they are on display in their home. The translucent windows facing the auto court provide privacy, while the opaque wood door confers a sense of security to the entrance.

a trellis and pergolas. As in any good entertainment space there are separate but linked spaces for dining, relaxing, and activities.

## Garage Conversion

Thanks to the dimensions of the huge gas-guzzling cars of the 1960s, the existing two-car garage and workroom was large enough to create a bedroom, bath, study, and walk-in closet. The study, located between the bedroom and the closet, has a window wall too. One great thing about this away space is its dimensions. It is big enough for a desk, built-in filing cabinets, and bookshelves, making a place for all those items that usually end up on either side of the bed. But it is not so large that it becomes a guest room or a repository for all the things you can't find a home for.

The large window walls of the bathroom and bedroom provide a private view of the patio and the hills above the house, while the mirrored wall in the bathroom both reflects the landscape and bounces light back

**Built-in storage** and lots of it is a key to the sleek, no-clutter look. The built-ins in this bathroom are several different sizes, with deep drawers for large towels and laundry to small drawers for toiletries. More than just a cliché, *A place for everything and everything in its place* is a golden rule for useful storage.

into the room. When Pat and Herb wake up to the view of hawks soaring over the large oak trees, it's hard to believe that the home is in Los Angeles, the second-largest city in the United States.

## Opening the Plan

In the remodeled house, the plan is virtually transparent, with one room flowing effortlessly into another. The minute you step into the house you are invited to the pool and patio area. Pat and Herb wanted all the living spaces, indoors and out, to be unified. This meant that the quiet rooms—bedrooms and bathrooms—would be hidden from view.

To reinforce the idea of an open plan, all full-height walls that separated the active rooms—living, dining, kitchen, and patio—were removed or made as transparent as possible with the generous use of glass. The new windows throughout the house repeat the square grid of the old windows to reinforce the sense of seamless design. To make the rooms look and feel larger, the ceiling was removed and the rafters exposed. The strong direction of the rafters points the eye to the outside walls.

Refacing a fireplace is one sure way to create a new look. The once dark, flat fireplace wall was boxed out in drywall to create the appearance of a sculpted hood,

**Wood finishes** can greatly affect the spatial quality of a room. The "basketball" floor finish is bright, shiny, and reflective, drawing attention to the floor by emphasizing the variation in the color of the wood. The more subtle satin finish of the rafters and ceiling decking catches the light in an atmospheric manner. The black-and-white sculptural fireplace adds a note of sophistication.

Before

Master bedroom

Kitchen

Garage

Bedroom

Dining room

Entry

Living room

Office

Dining/family room

Pool

Kitchen

Walk-in closet

Master bedroom

Bedroom

Carport

Entry

Living room

After

and the face was resurfaced with elegant black stone. The color palette of the living space is very spare, with white walls and white furnishings. An all-white scheme can be intimidating or cold, but the choice of natural finish for the wood floors and ceiling bestows the rooms with a warm and relaxed atmosphere. The couple's art collection and the views of the landscape provide additional color.

# Stretching the Envelope

ABOVE, **The contemporary, taut** steel-and-wood banister stands in stark contrast to the more traditional detailing of the built-in wood cabinetry throughout the house.

FACING PAGE, **Finishes are important** in conveying the tone of the room. Choosing to combine dark cherry cabinets, slate flooring, heavy granite countertops, and red oak flooring creates a classic adult look. Oatmeal cookies, milk, and sippy cups are welcome at snack time, but after hours the mood is suited to cocktails, canapés, and crystal.

I F YOU'RE INVOLVED IN A REMODELING PROJECT, there may come a point in the design process when you have to ask yourself which is more important, the integrity of the house style or how your family defines home? Mark and Ruth Ellen's 1960s vintage Minnesota Ranch was a typical contractor one-story Ranch with a shoebox plan. The house had some nice features—a large picture window with sidelights, slider windows in the bedroom, wood shakes below the eave line, horizontal wood siding above, and a stone chimney—but it lacked sparkle. It could have been anyone's home.

## Here to Stay

The starting point for the remodeling was Mark and Ruth Ellen's intention that this was the house they would live in well into their old age. This decision freed them to design a house suited to their own particular taste, instead of playing it safe with a neutral fix-up for quick resale. They didn't go wild with off-the-wall ideas, but they did make some big-ticket decisions. Excavating a new basement and raising the roof for an eventual second story are things they probably wouldn't have considered if they were planning to move.

**Unless the project** is a complete makeover, it's best to use materials massing that reflect the original house. Here, the addition built on the character and materials of the original house, preserving the gable ends.

A long-term commitment means that the cost of the remodeling will be amortized over their lifetime and the remodeling can be done in phases as finances and family schedules allow.

## What They Said

One atypical aspect of Ruth Ellen and Mark's Ranch is that it didn't have the usual open, free flow of movement. Even though the house was almost 2,000 sq. ft., the family felt constricted. They called on Tim Fuller of SALA Architects to help them with their remodeling ideas. Tim identified several key issues they needed to think about. First, which rooms worked well for the family? Operating under the assumption that if it's not broken, don't fix it, the family agreed that the two front bedrooms, the bathroom, and closets were fine just the

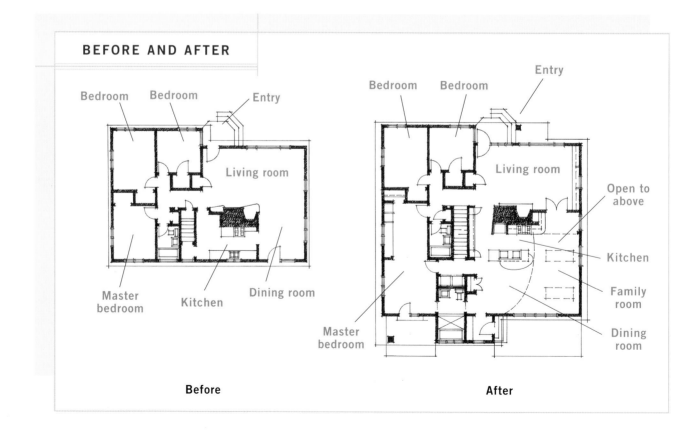

**BEFORE AND AFTER**

Before

Bedroom  Bedroom  Entry
Living room
Master bedroom  Kitchen  Dining room

After

Bedroom  Bedroom  Entry
Living room
Open to above
Kitchen
Family room
Master bedroom
Dining room

**Both the master bedroom** and the family room have access to outdoor patios, by simply projecting the entry bay, a privacy screen is created between the intimate and the shared family outdoor spaces.

**Digging a huge hole** in your backyard, building a new foundation, and ripping the roof off are not projects for the faint-hearted. But neither is house hunting and moving.

**The family room** is the heart of this house. The furniture can be rearranged any number of ways, to accommodate a crowd for a holiday party or for a family evening alone. Even the entertainment center is on wheels.

way they were. And the basement stair enclosure was in the right location for the planned second-floor expansion.

Second, Tim challenged them to think about what was in the wrong place and what was missing. The family wanted a family room on the first floor, convenient to the kitchen, the patio, and the backyard. The original kitchen was little more than a galley, and it felt disconnected from the rest of the family living spaces. And what is a remodeling without complexity and contradiction? Mark and Ruth Ellen wanted their home to have a feeling of free-flowing family togetherness and plenty of opportunities for quiet and private spaces.

**The new roof** configuration allows the introduction of skylights into the bedroom ceiling. The bedroom has its own private covered patio accessible through the double French doors, great for views and cross-ventilation.

## What They Meant

Sometimes the thing an architect does best is listen. While Ruth Ellen and Mark were discussing their house, Tim kept hearing a tone of disappointment, contrasted with Mark's excited tone when he spoke of the time he lived in a loft space. It was obvious to the architect that the couple wanted to capture the dramatic feeling of loft living in a home suited for family life. He threw out the idea: Why not introduce a loft into the Ranch? The couple wanted both family and private spaces, and with the slope of the site and the configuration of the lot they had two choices: Go up or build a large addition to the back. The yard was important to the family, and they didn't want the Ranch to become a Rambler and take up all the yard space. Other homes in the neighborhood are two stories, so adding gables would actually bring their house more into the character of the neighborhood.

## What They Did

The final plan added another 630 sq. ft. of living space to the first floor and the same amount of storage and work space to the basement. For now, the second floor is a mezzanine that soars over the family room, its edgy and contemporary detailing sending a clear message that life in a Ranch can be full of surprises. The master bedroom suite is scheduled for phase two.

A hallmark of Ranch design is that one element does double duty. The mezzanine acts as ceiling for the kitchen, the lowered ceiling providing a sense of enclosure without shutting the kitchen off from the double-height family room. Now that the family can see the

Because the homeowners were thinking ahead to
"aging in place," they considered what kind of
appliances and hardware would be best, and they
located the laundry on the first floor, convenient
to the bedrooms and baths.

A unique look doesn't have to be more expensive. The
architect chose to use standard super-sized 16 x 16 flooring tile on the walls, and with fewer joints the room
appears larger. The tub surround tiles are 4 x 16, which
provides a horizontal counterpoint.

backyard from all the active living rooms, the addition
seems much bigger than it actually is.

## Eclectic Interiors

One likely reason for the popularity of the Ranch style
is that homeowners like the fact that it does not conform to any one style or period. Old and new can be
mingled together. In this house, the kitchen combines
an industrial aesthetic of exposed steel I-beams and
high-tech lighting with handcrafted cherry Mission
cabinets. The study is traditionally styled with built-in
oak cabinetry, while the bathroom is cutting-edge
Euro style: The hand-held shower drains directly into a
floor drain, and transparent floor-to-ceiling plate-glass
shower doors separate the shower and tub from the rest
of the bathroom. The combining of different styles may
make some architects and interior designers shudder,
but an aesthetic mix can express the unique personalities that make up a family.

Ruth Ellen and Mark's home is tiptoeing into the
category of complete makeover, but until the second-
floor bedroom is built it is still a one-story house with
a double-height space. The design is flexible, the house
looks complete now, and the skylights in the new roof
flood the room with light and remove all traces of the
constricted feeling that the family didn't like. When and
if they enclose the second-floor bedroom, it will fit in
seamlessly—just the way original Ranch expansions
were intended to.

**In the future,** the family might have use for a formal living room, but for the time being, most of the entertaining takes place in the family room and the backyard. The living room can be easily closed off from the active areas by two glass-fronted French doors. For now, the built-in bookshelves and desk accommodate a quiet study.

# CHAPTER FOUR

# RANCH MAKEOVERS

ABOVE, **It's easy** to understand why Ranch houses were nicknamed Ramblers in some parts of the country. Designed to be added on to, Ranches could ramble across the landscape in any direction.

FACING PAGE, **You would have** to be a forensic architect to uncover the Ranch in this now English country manor. Makeovers that are well done leave little evidence of their former style.

For half a century, the ranch style has dominated the residential landscape. Just as many baby boomers of the same vintage are not ready to fade quietly into obscurity, neither is the Ranch. Many Ranch houses are getting a second wind, a total makeover, and like the baby boomers who grew up in them, they're in better shape now than they ever were.

You may well wonder whether houses that now look more like English country homes, farmhouses, and French cottages should really be in a book on Ranch homes. Of course! Just as many a New Yorker started life as a Hoosier, a basic Ranch house can be remodeled into whatever style the homeowner wants. In this chapter, you'll see examples of Ranch homes whose only charm may have been their location transformed into a wide variety of architectural expressions. In an odd twist, the very fact that many of these homes began as plain and ordinary "Ranchburgers" is exactly the reason they are great makeover candidates. Because some of

# Through a Dark Glass Lightly

**FIFTEEN YEARS** ago we designed an extensive remodel that included a clear glass sliding shower door in a new master bath. The plumber thought clear glass immodest and substituted darkened smoked glass (and had to replace it at his own expense). Today, clear glass, natural light, and expanded vistas are all part of the residential scene . . . even in the bathroom.

Up-to-date bathrooms employ glass as a functional separator of environments, not as a visual barrier. European glazing techniques along with minimal framing and clear sealants have made a transparent material ever more transparent.

Using glass can make any space seem larger yet still allow you to separate uses. With the advent of master bathrooms for adults only, there is less need for internal privacy. Innovations in glass allow for a multitude of finishes, colors, textures, and fritted or silk-screened patterns that can impart varying degrees of "obscured" glazing.

the homes in this chapter were built on the foundations of existing Ranches, they are not teardowns. Some could be considered "wraparounds" because they incorporate parts of the existing plan, or "buildups" because they incorporate the first floor of the original home.

## From Grand to Bland, and Back Again

In the mid-1960s, Sunday newspaper's real estate sections were filled with news of "grand openings" of model homes in brand-new suburbs, and most of the new homes were of the Ranch style. Each new suburb tried to outdo earlier ones, as houses came with new features: swimming pools, sunken living rooms with pit fireplaces, sound systems, security, and intercom systems. Housing styles responded more to consumer demands for "new, bigger, better" than they did to regional or

ABOVE AND FACING PAGE, **Losing a few walls** and highlighting the home's good bone structure with a new color scheme gives an old Ranch (bottom photo, facing page) a new lease on life.

In the 1960s this house had all the latest design options. Large picture windows, brick fireplace, vertical wood siding, an exposed-aggregate patio, and a fiberglass roof insert over the porch were all the accepted vocabulary of residential architecture. Although it was a much-loved family home, it could have been built anywhere.

Because of its age, even a classic Ranch is going to require a certain amount of makeover. Aging mechanical systems and out-of-date kitchens are almost a sure bet.

climatic context. Whether they were in Georgia, Maryland, North Carolina, New York, or Minnesota, "Contractor Contemporaries" all began to all look pretty much the same. The excitement about the Ranch style was beginning to wear thin—there were just too many of them; they weren't special any longer.

Somewhere along the line, builders forgot that this housing type was intended to express the individual interests of the families who inhabited it. And, as millions of single-story Ranch-like homes spread out over the landscape, the home buyers forgot it too. The Ranch was no longer an innovative house; it was just affordable and plentiful.

## THE RANCH RIDES AGAIN

At first we thought it was a Milwaukee phenomenon, but we have discovered that it happens all across the country. People grow up in Ranch houses, go off to explore the world, come back home, and buy the house they grew up in from their parents (or buy from their parents' friends). There's one such example in this chapter (see pp. 146–151). But when the "children" return home, they are not content to move back into their

# Phantom Ranch

☆ **WHILE SOME** Ranch owners look to preserve at least part of the house's heritage, others see the humble Ranch as a *tabula rasa* on which to draw their own dreams of home. For the owners of this Connecticut home, the dream was to transform a Ranch into a farmhouse. The project required taking down the entire house except for one wall in the front and the living room situated in the back. Most of the foundation remained, though a small portion was removed so the basement could be turned into an in-law apartment.

With so much of the existing house gone, the obvious question is, why save any of the original at all? From the architect's perspective, the foundation, basement, and remaining walls were worth keeping and building up and around. Besides, the footprint of the house was something to work off of and the siting was perfect. As for many Ranch owners, the lot was more valuable for its real estate than for its architecture.

childhood bedrooms. They are more likely to move the bedroom, raise the roof, add a second floor, and while they're at it, double the square footage.

## GOOD BONES

As we saw in chapter 2, there's a demand for classic Ranches that have all the hallmarks intact. But there are thousands upon thousands of cookie-cutter Ranches that are too small and too dated to attract today's home buyer. Due to the age of the homes, it's highly probable that many will have a fair amount of deferred maintenance. As you go house hunting, you will find no dearth of brick-and-wood three-bedroom, one-and-a-half-bath Ranches with aging roofs, obsolete mechanical systems, and tired interior design. The good news is that many of these homes were well built and well sited and are located in desirable neighborhoods. A recurring theme we heard from the homeowners who completely made over their Ranches was that the house had good bones.

## FIRST THINGS FIRST

Unless you are a design professional, it may be difficult for you to envision how you make a Ranch house over into another style. The key is to involve a design professional as early as possible in the process. Not every Ranch has makeover potential. If you live in a large metropolitan area, you might be able to find firms that specialize in total renovation of older homes into different styles. Ask people who have done projects similar to what you are contemplating for references.

After a design consultation, you might be advised to build new or tear down the existing house. There are so many issues to work with simultaneously that you'll be justified in seeking professional advice. Chances are that if you buy a house you don't like and you later find it is not right for your conversion plans, it will prove to be

**There are thousands** of "contractor contemporaries" in the suburbs of most major cities. Overlooked as too small, too dark, and in need of updating from the furnace to the roof, these homes may be priced right for total makeovers.

very difficult to resell. And remember, even though the Ranch itself might be a bargain, a major construction project takes time, patience, money, flexibility, attention to details, and a sense of humor.

## WHAT TO LOOK FOR

If you decide to look for a Ranch to make over, you have a different mindset than if you were going to build a new house or live in the house with no intention of remodeling. Because you're not going to tear the house down and build new, you have to accept that certain elements cannot be altered without incurring major expenses. The most critical thing to determine is that the foundation is sound. This is one instance where it is imperative to take along an engineer or an architect to do the inspection, especially if you want to add a second floor.

If you plan to dramatically alter the house, don't concern yourself with existing color schemes or the window treatments—look at the Ranch for its makeover possibilities. Ask important questions if you are considering revising the plan: Where are the structural walls located? Where is the plumbing? What about the house is worth saving? Is the fireplace in the right place? Can the garage be converted into living space? If so, is the lot large enough that a new garage can be built within the setback? Can you live with the existing exterior materials? If not, can they be altered?

At open houses people spend lots of time in basements looking at the mechanical systems. You may be better off if you factor in the expense of updating heating and air-conditioning. New systems are both smaller and more energy efficient than older ones. If you hobble along with an old system you may save some up-front costs, but odds are that you'll face the inconvenience and expense of a failing older furnace. And if

our experience is typical, odds are even better that this failure will occur on the eve of a major holiday.

## GREAT LOCATION

Second only to good bones, great location is the major reason to buy a Ranch house. Keep in mind that the lot and the neighboring properties impact your decision to buy and make over as much as the house itself. There are several things to think about as you view the property:

✧ Is it large enough to graciously accommodate a major addition?

**If you're updating** a brick Ranch, be sure to consult with an expert about the best way to treat brick. Brick has a natural water-repellent finish, and under no circumstances should that seal be broken. If it is compromised, you could be in for some very costly repairs.

**A classic hallmark** of the Ranch style is the use of three or more exterior materials, with little or no direct relationship between them. In the 1950s and '60s, the materials were usually brick, stone, and painted plywood paneling. Today the plywood remains, but new materials such as Drivit and metals are prevalent.

◇ How will the slope of the site affect costs?

◇ Is there a great view that a second-floor addition could capture?

◇ Can you add on without losing mature trees?

◇ What opportunities are there for outdoor rooms?

Turn your attention to the neighboring houses. What style are they? If they are all small single-story Ranches, a grand two-story English Country home may look out of place. If there are other grand makeovers in the neighborhood, then your plans for a total redo will fit right in. Contact the municipality to obtain accurate information concerning the setback

## Why You Need a Survey

**SEVERAL YEARS AGO** we were hired to design a master bedroom suite addition to an existing Ranch. At the start of each project we always request the existing surveys, drawings, and any other pertinent information bearing on permits and regulations. The client, a realtor, insisted that he could locate the property line for us and indicated that a survey would not be needed until later. Unfortunately, when the survey was finally executed, it showed that the homeowner was wrong and the proposed addition would not fit.

A survey is one of the most important drawings you'll have done of your house. Titled "Plat of Survey," the drawing will include the name of your street along with the property lines that define your lot and will locate any existing construction. Adjacent fences and properties may be notated in reference to your home, and overhead power lines, underground water lines, and even larger trees may also be shown. Two words to watch for: An *easement* is a limited use of your property that may be granted to a power company to run lines overhead, while a *covenant* is a lease that may be granted to a neighbor for use of a shared driveway.

**Inlaid wood floors,** faux painting, and fleur-de-lys sconces are not standard fare in most Ranch interiors, but in a total makeover you can be as eclectic as you wish.

requirements, the allowed ratio of built to unbuilt area allowed, and other requirements before you start your plans.

## COMMON COMPLAINTS

Almost every original house in this chapter was described by its owners as too dark, too small, and as having an awkward floor plan and no indoor-outdoor relationship. These were certainly not pedigree Ranches, which are all about an open plan, lots of light,

and a terrific indoor-outdoor relationship. In addition, the homeowners were not committed to the Ranch style; they wanted homes with a different aesthetic sensibility. As you will see in the following examples, if you look for opportunities rather than constraints, you can really go in any direction you wish, either borrowing from the past or peering into the future.

# Capturing the View

I N PACIFIC PALISADES, CALIFORNIA, views often make or break the value of a property. Views of the ocean are at a premium, as are those of the Santa Monica mountains. These views are not only jealously guarded but they are protected by law. When Rosanne and Don decided to expand her 1950s Ranch house to make room for a blended family, the shape of the 1,600-sq.-ft. addition was dictated in large part by the need to preserve their neighbor's view of the ocean. Don, now a writer, was a builder at the time, and he called in architect Paul Murdoch to be a member of the design team.

To complicate matters further, the irregular geometry of the lot placed even more restrictions on where and how the major addition could be grafted onto the existing 3,000-sq.-ft. home. The couple wanted the new addition to contrast with the existing building but in a harmonious and inconspicuous way. Rosanne originally bought the house because she liked its rustic charm, and it was important to her that the makeover retain that feeling.

Contrary to the ideal California Ranch house, the original 1950s builder home did not take advantage of

**To meet height restrictions,** the new addition had to be 3 ft. lower than the original house. The lower level feels private, even though it is visually connected. The consistent use of the wood cabinetry weaves the new and the old together.

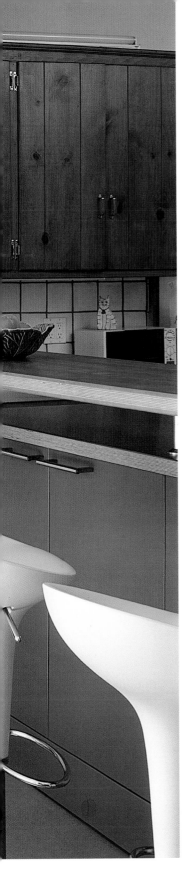

**Close to the curb,** the only way this quaint shingled 1950s Ranch could expand was up and to the rear. The new addition captures views of the ocean and mountains that the original home turned its back on.

ocean and mountain views. The interior of the home was dark and compartmentalized, and the gardens were barely visible from inside. The main goal for the addition was to create rooms that comfortably allow a wide variety of experiences, from large parties to quiet family relaxing. Included on the "wish list" was a master bedroom suite, a study/home office, and another bedroom and bath. Outdoor rooms, with easy inside-outside connections, were also high on the list.

The new rear two-story addition is built right up to the limit of the setback line. A total of 1,000 sq. ft. of the original house was demolished in order to build a more efficient and attractive family room that has a free-flowing connection to the patio. The new first-floor bedroom enjoys a ground floor connection and privacy.

**The minimal use** of materials and colors, such as the horizontal copper band topping the fireplace wall, brings out the warmth of the natural wood and mimics the warm glint of dying embers.

**Cork and concrete floors** are both enjoying renewed popularity. Cork is a great insulator, highly resilient, and a good choice if you are interested in sustainable building materials. Concrete is high-style and low-maintenance.

## A New Profile

One of the biggest challenges in any addition is designing a new roof that is compatible with the old one. On this house, the ridge height of the existing roof could not be raised because it would block the neighbor's view of the ocean. The space under the roof was actually a low attic—there wasn't sufficient floor-to-floor height for a full-height bedroom. Paul's solution was to regrade the backyard so that the new first floor of the addition is 3 ft. lower than the original first floor. This allowed the necessary overall height for the addition without blocking views. Since most of the homes in this area are single story, sinking the addition into the site helped conceal the second story from the street.

## Fruit Smoothie

California is known for setting trends in fashion, foods, and fads. In recent years, one trend, the smoothie—a concoction of fruit, juices, and yogurt—has enjoyed coast-to-coast popularity. Although the combinations may sound odd, they taste delicious because of the way they blend together. Creating a seamless whole out of two projects built 50 years apart can pose similar challenges. The projects were blended together with a new exterior "skin." The simple yet rich palette of gray-green smooth troweled-finish cement plaster replaced the board-and-batten wood siding of the original exterior. The new two-story addition in the back is clad in mahogany wood with a copper fascia. The indoor-outdoor connection is celebrated with colored concrete patios that flow directly inside, creating a transition to dark cork flooring.

To cast out the shadows and bring in more light, sliding doors and floor-to-ceiling windows were added, and the wood decking of the ceiling was painted white. The beams, window, and door frames are natural wood. The new fireplace wall floats below the ceiling, enabling the library wall beyond to peek above the top of the fireplace. Most of the interior is painted white—using one color unifies the rooms and showcases the natural woods and the owners' collection of pottery. Throughout the house, custom-designed built-ins save floor space while creating a one-of-a-kind atmosphere.

**The generously scaled** handcrafted hardware immediately tells company that this is a special house that welcomes guests. Instead of going overboard on detailing and ornamentation, the honest planks of the door express the essence of wood.

## BEFORE AND AFTER

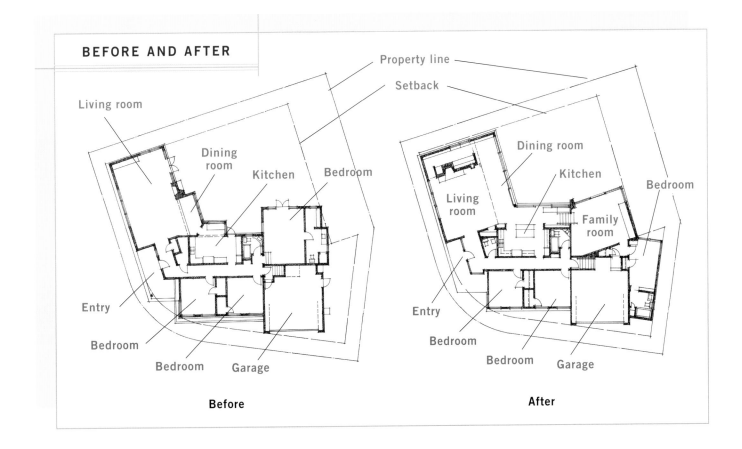

Before

After

# Out to Pasture

ABOVE, **The original patio** was well built and well located, but it wasn't particularly interesting. Adding the trellis and creating an arbor transforms a drab patio into an outdoor room, with vertical and overhead definition.

FACING PAGE, **In the addition,** the original living room, with a fireplace, became the dining room. The couple added a second fireplace in the new family room. Putting fireplaces back-to-back may mean that they can share a flue or a gas line and save you money.

L INDA, A WEAVER, LIVED IN her simple brick Maryland Ranch house before she married Roger. The 10 acres of pastureland are an idyllic setting for her dogs, goats, and llamas. The two-bedroom, one-and-a-half-bath house was comfortable for one but less than perfect for two. Both Linda and Roger liked the scale and livability of this Ranch and saw a makeover as a great opportunity to express their own aesthetic: one of elegance and craft.

## Shuffling the Deck

The beauty of this project is that the architects, Bruce Finkelstein and Kitty Daly from HBF + Architects, saw many possibilities in the existing house. Almost all the structure of the original house remains (as well as the plumbing and exterior cladding), though the various rooms have been shuffled around. Retaining as much of the house as possible allowed the couple to spend dollars on critical design decisions that would make a dramatic difference and still stay within the budget.

The Ranch was a classic "H" plan. The architects suggested filling in an interior corner of the "H" to expand the newly configured kitchen, family, and dining rooms, but a problem that many makeovers face

The original double-gabled brick Ranch was compact and inward looking, more suited to an urban block than 10 beautiful acres in rural Maryland.

popped up. How can a new roof meet the old roof in an attractive (and leakproof) manner? In this instance, the architects proposed that the addition be a one-and-a-half-story room, and happily this proved to be the right answer for a variety of concerns. On the exterior, the increased height prevents the house from appearing too long and low. On the interior, the taller element allows for different ceiling heights and windows, and natural light now streams into the house throughout the day.

## Practically Beautiful

Connections to the outdoors were particularly important to Roger and Linda. With the newly configured plan, they can go directly to outdoor rooms from the

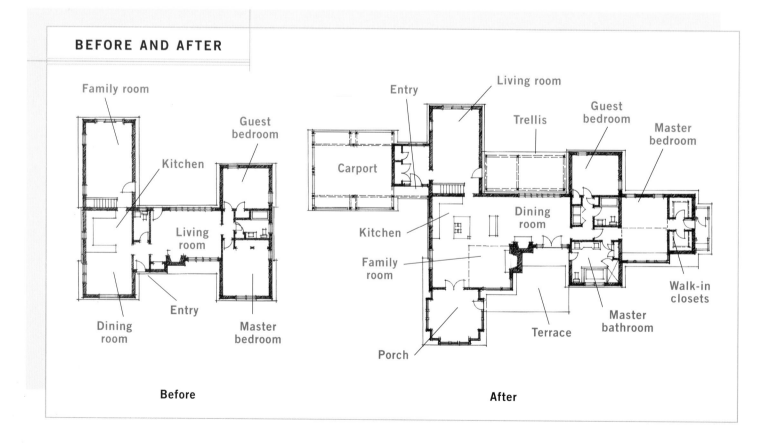

**BEFORE AND AFTER**

Before

After

dining room, the enclosed porch, the master bath, and their bedroom. They even built an outdoor shower-stall pavilion directly outside the walk-in closet in their bedroom, where they can clean up after working in the pasture and avoid tracking mud into the house.

The original house didn't have a garage—Linda parked on a gravel driveway. The couple were concerned that the mass of a two-car garage located in front of their home would destroy the small scale, one characteristic that they were emphatic about retaining. They were also reluctant to spend a large part of their budget on something that they were not particularly enthusiastic about. Keeping economy and scale in mind, the architects designed what is, in fact, a two-car carport, but appears to be a two-car garage. The simple post-and-beam construction has screen walls that are

**The large addition,** on the right was stepped back from the main house so that its presence wouldn't be overwhelming.

**Years ago outdoor showers** were common, a practical response to the fact that outdoor work was dirty. Today they are showing up in renovations across the country but with a little more whimsy and delight than purely utilitarian needs would dictate.

**High-style pendant** lights cast a warm glow over the granite-topped kitchen island and lend a certain formality to a utilitarian work surface.

**Whether your lot is** 10 acres or a half-acre, consider ways to incorporate the landscape into the entry sequence. A sloping site offers opportunities for retaining walls and steps to fashion grade change that provides a graceful entrance with planting beds.

open at the top, while wood grillwork and board-and-batten wood siding are suspended between the support posts. The twin gables and the siding materials match the single gable of the outdoor shower pavilion, tying all parts of the new addition together.

## A First Impression

Our clients are often surprised when we suggest that one way to greatly improve the flow of their house is to move the front entry. Somehow, relocating the front door always seems to be a radical suggestion, but it's certainly far less radical (and less expensive) than raising a roof, something most people seem to accept more easily as a reasonable solution to acquire additional useable square footage.

Rob and Linda's property is picturesque, but the old approach to the house ignored the setting. When guests arrived, they parked their cars and literally bumped into the house. Relocating the entry allowed the guests to enjoy an attractive arrival sequence, up flagstone steps, past native plantings, around a gently curved walkway into a proper foyer. The house gives the impression that it is larger than it is because the landscape is the first "great room" the guests enter. The new foyer greets the guests in true Ranch manner, with twin sidelights flanking the door, and you can see all the way through the foyer to the backyard.

**The dormer over** the entry adds a grace note of familiarity to a relaxed house, while the expanse of glass and distant outdoor view makes the room appear larger than it really is.

# All in the Family

ABOVE, **Finely detailed woodwork** is a hallmark of this neo-Craftsman Ranch renovation. The architect calls the wood trim that surrounds the glass-block interior windows a "water table" trim band, a term more commonly applied to an exterior trim detail.

FACING PAGE, **Outdoor eating spaces** are located on the spacious deck just outside the door of the breakfast room, but for those days when heavy raindrops fall from gathering storm clouds, the low windows provide a panoramic view of the changing colors of the Sound.

J AYNE'S CHILDHOOD HOME WAS A CLASSIC 1960s one-story Ranch and carport, with a low horizontal profile and wood siding over a brick-veneer base. Located near Tacoma, Washington, the home has breathtaking views of Puget Sound and Point Defiance Park. In the past 10 years, the area has experienced intense development pressure, and Jayne's mother wanted to keep the house in the family. Jayne and her husband, Gene, bought the home and, with her mother's enthusiastic support, began an extensive exterior and interior makeover from Ranch to Craftsman Shingle Style, working with architect Brett Drager of Drager Gould Architects.

## Open to Formality

The couple wanted a more formal lifestyle and more richly appointed rooms than the Ranch style afforded. They were careful to borrow selectively from the Craftsman style without slavishly mimicking it. Because they didn't tear the house down to the foundation, they needed to acknowledge some Ranch characteristics and integrate them into the renovation.

We have all seen homes where the owners impose a decorating scheme that just doesn't work with the style

**The exterior is flanked** by a long deck that creates multiple options for sun seekers and shade dwellers to enjoy.

of the house. In this house, the slanted tongue-and-groove wood ceiling says "Ranch," while the brightly painted white woodwork combines with a neutral color scheme for the walls to tie all the rooms together. The detailing—compound baseboards, expressed pilasters, interior windows with mullions, and wood trim—all reach back in history, but the end result is a clean and contemporary expression. Ironically, cutting openings in the walls to allow views from one room to another made the plan more open than when it was a Ranch.

## Giant Steps

If you plan to live in your home for a generation (or in this case two), big moves that will make you happier tend to be worth it. Nothing is worse than completing a remodeling project and 10 years later lamenting that you were penny-wise and pound-foolish.

Jayne and Gene took some pretty giant steps. They enclosed a porch and raised the roof to expand the kitchen; lifted the roof over the living room and added a stair to create a second-floor master suite; relocated several plumbing walls; removed a fireplace; added a fireplace; and clad the house totally in cedar shingles. These were not frivolous decisions. The only way to gain more square footage was to go up. The neighborhood is serviced by septic systems, and the land available for construction was limited by the footprint of their septic field.

Not that they built higher only for practical purposes—they also wanted a good-looking house. Lifting the roof above the new kitchen and breakfast

# Roof Lines

**ranch style**

**EVEN IF** you don't live in a Prairie style Ranch, your Ranch home still emphasizes the horizontal, primarily through the strength of gable, hip, or shed roofs. And because Ranches are so horizontal, the roof element is in large part responsible for the look of your home.

Adding onto a Ranch roof can be a real challenge, because the existing pitch and clearance above the windows may not allow you to extend the roof pitch at the low point. Depending on your situation, the new roof can run perpendicular to the existing roof, it can mirror the existing roof, it can extend from the high point, or it can even attach with a slightly different pitch. A visit to a Ranch neighborhood will show that all these examples can work, in part because the Ranch's low horizontal nature conceals what would otherwise be a fussy transition.

**The small windows** in the master bedroom are deep-set, while the tall windows are flush with the interior wall. Details like this make a room more alive, animating the architectural elements.

**The library is** an interior room without any windows to the exterior; a skylight cut into the roof provides natural light.

nook creates balance and livens up the façade. The new double-gabled roof completes the transformation from Ranch to Craftsman. The gray cedar shingles unify the new additions with the old house and fit into the shore landscape much more harmoniously than the brick-and-wood siding of the original home did.

Two of the most dramatic steps the owners took were to remove two fireplaces. The double fireplace in the old family room is now framed into the wall. The old fireplace in the former living room/dining room blocked the best view of the Sound; it was torn out and replaced with French doors to improve the indoor-outdoor connection and enhance the view. The new gas-insert fireplace is tucked into the library, giving a room without exterior views a warm focal point.

## BEFORE AND AFTER

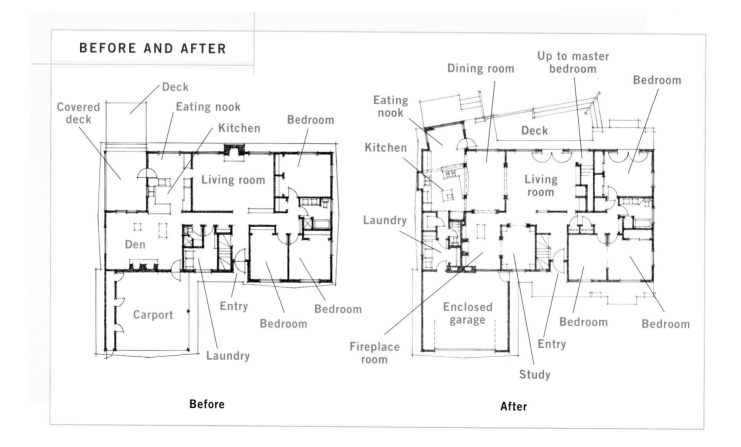

**Before**

**After**

You might wonder whether it would have been easier for Jayne and Gene just to tear the whole thing down and start over. If you look closely at the plans, you'll see that the majority of the original home's structure is intact. The first-floor bedroom and bath wing were updated. The two guest bedrooms now have the flexibility to be one large room or a suite, depending on whether the pocket doors are open or closed. The architect was adamant about retaining as much as possible of the existing house in order to stay within budget and be able to take the big steps that create, as they say in the movies, "a suspension of disbelief."

**Large sections of** interior walls were removed to improve the flow of circulation, and interior windows were inserted to offer a play of light in the rooms that didn't have a water view. The glass block emphasizes the thickness of the walls and the quality of construction.

# TV Dinner
# to Fusion Cuisine

ABOVE, **Sturdy arched timbers** at the peaks of the gables and over the front door, wood shakes, and clinker brick combine to create a family home that is as welcoming as a North Woods lodge. The stepping of the rooflines creates an intimate scale for a very large home.

FACING PAGE, **A formal foyer** and music room were carved out of the long and skinny living room. The fireplace is the one remnant of the original house. Family members use the music room as an away space—a quiet place to talk, gaze into the fire, or practice their scales.

T HE FIRM OF MORRIS–DAY DESIGNERS AND BUILDERS in Arlington, Virginia, has established an excellent reputation for taking tired cookie-cutter Ranch houses and completely transforming them, both spatially and stylistically. This home, and the one that follows (see pp. 158–163), both in McLean, Virginia, were in dire need of some architectural expertise.

## The Lodge

The Ranch had been neglected for many years before the current owners stumbled upon it while jogging. It was too small, too run down, and not at all what they were looking for—but the setting was idyllic. The back of the lot had views of protected parkland, a creek, and woods. The neighborhood was developed at the end of World War I as a summer colony (many of the now large homes started out as cottages and cabins). Property values were rising quickly, as homes were bought and gut-rehabbed. The couple decided to take the plunge and talked to architect Dwight McNeil of Morris-Day about the property's potential.

Every family is unique, so it follows that every residential solution should also be unique. Sometimes it's as basic as a simple physical characteristic: in this case, all

## FIRST AND SECOND FLOOR

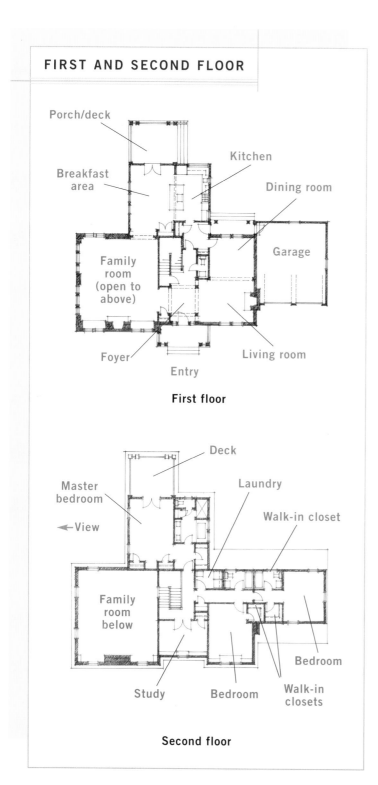

**First floor**

*(Labels: Porch/deck, Kitchen, Breakfast area, Dining room, Family room (open to above), Garage, Foyer, Living room, Entry)*

**Second floor**

*(Labels: Deck, Master bedroom, Laundry, View, Walk-in closet, Family room below, Study, Bedroom, Walk-in closets, Bedroom)*

the members of the family are quite tall. In fact, one reason the owners were on the lookout for a new home was that the charming farmhouse they were living in had such low ceilings that one of the children had to kneel to brush her teeth. Their priorities were spacious rooms that reflected their casual lifestyle and a getaway space for each member of the family. Dwight brought up the idea of using a lodge as an architectural precedent, and the family liked it. They talked about what "lodge" meant to them, and they came up with a list that included rustic materials, large gathering spaces for kids and adults, fireplaces, connection to the woods, and, of course, a guest bedroom.

## Down to the Foundation

After a careful evaluation of the existing home, the decision was made to take the house down to the foundation, retaining only the fireplace, the location of the front door, and the basement. Everything else went. The original home was less than 1,500 sq. ft., the three bed-

**Like many ordinary Ranches,** the existing home was located in a wonderful neighborhood and had great potential for a total transformation of style.

LEFT, **Just making a room big** doesn't make it impressive. Stepping the brick-dust red walls slightly behind the wood wall paneling makes the walls appear to be very thick and solid, a necessary impression in a two-story room with an abundance of windows.

BELOW, **A limited palette** of colors and materials allows the house to fit comfortably within the landscape. The rich chocolate brown of the wood trim responds to the wooded site, while the ivory tone of the siding provides a canvas for leafy shadows.

rooms were tiny, and the two bathrooms had the best view of the parkland. The house had been neglected for so long that there was little worth saving.

The couple's plans were ambitious. On the first floor, they added 480 sq. ft. for a kitchen/breakfast room with covered connections to a porch and a new two-car garage. The former bedroom wing was transformed into a two-story-high family room that is so generous in all dimensions, windows, woodwork, and furnishings that it does recreate the warm feeling of hospitality you get when you enter a well-appointed lodge.

# Every Kitchen Has an Island

**THOUGH** the poet John Donne wrote, "No man is an island," it seems that just about every Ranch kitchen has one. The kitchen island and its cousin the peninsula have been popular fixtures in the Ranch kitchen since its formative years, and they are still going strong.

Most Ranch islands or peninsulas began as an expansion of storage and work surfaces that brought the food preparation "out" into a more social setting. As appliances, storage, serving, and dining opportunities grow, the island becomes a social center for the kitchen and consequently the entire home.

If you are considering replacing, updating, or just plain reconfiguring the island, there are some important issues. Will your island house a cooktop, a double sink, a cutting board, or a half-refrigerator? Will the island provide the occasional buffet for guests at an adjacent dining table, or will the family eat breakfast there on high stools or low dining chairs? Adding appliances or fixtures will require running services to the island. Sinks need vent stacks, while ranges need to be vented either through a hood above or through the floor.

Multiple tasks can be accomplished with design flair: A raised counter for informal dining will also provide a backsplash for the sink or stove while hiding messy kitchen prep areas.

**Glass-fronted doors** lead into the children's study, located at the top of the stairs, overlooking the front drive. The kids are always connected to the pulse of the house.

## Over and Under

The new second floor has just over 2,000 sq. ft. of private family rooms. Each of three bedrooms has its own bath and walk-in closet, and the two children's bedrooms have cathedral ceilings (remember, these kids are tall!). A large porch looking out over the woodlands connects to the parents' bedroom. At the top of the stair, with a view over the front yard, the children share a study with back-to-back desks, built-in bookcases, and a window seat. Due to the sloped site, many of the basement rooms have large windows, creating a pleasant underground location for the sewing room, study, guest room, and recreation room. All in all, the owners have used every square inch of the house, new and old, to create a gracious and comfortable home that looks as though it has always been there.

**Covered connections** from the kitchen to the garage are always welcome, no matter how temperate the climate. The beaded-board ceiling helps reinforce the lodge imagery, inside and out.

# Learning
## to Relax

ABOVE, **The original Ranch** is tucked between the two new wings and behind the new bay window. The dove-gray horizontal siding gives the house a low-slung Craftsman look, a far cry from the little brick bunker it started life as.

FACING PAGE, **Having the garage** so close to the front door is convenient, but it can also be dangerous. The architect incorporated "preview" platforms to separate pedestrians from the driveway. The stepped deck and broad slate walkway are an elegant and safety-minded solution.

THE ORIGINAL 1,500-SQ.-FT. HOUSE that occupied this site might best be described as "uptight" (see the photo on p. 163). The *wannabe* Colonial Ranch was well constructed, and the variegated brick, ironwork trellis, gable ends, and faux shutters constituted an acceptable checklist of residential ornamentation, but it was clearly a house, not a home. The interiors were equally parsimonious, with low ceilings, minimal trim, and frugally dispersed windows. The house didn't exude the warmth and hospitality of a home that is comfortable in its own skin—or in its setting (perched on a gentle slope, the house is set back from the street with mature trees forming a lush backdrop rarely found in new subdivisions).

At least the house was well maintained, and much of the existing first-floor plan, while in need of updating, was incorporated in the makeover. If you're serious about staying on a set budget, it's a good idea not to relocate stairs, bathrooms, or kitchens, which are all easy to move around on paper but expensive to actually implement.

## Through the Roof

The roof needed to be replaced, which gave the owners the perfect opportunity to raise it. Lifting the roof changed the proportions of the building entirely, and

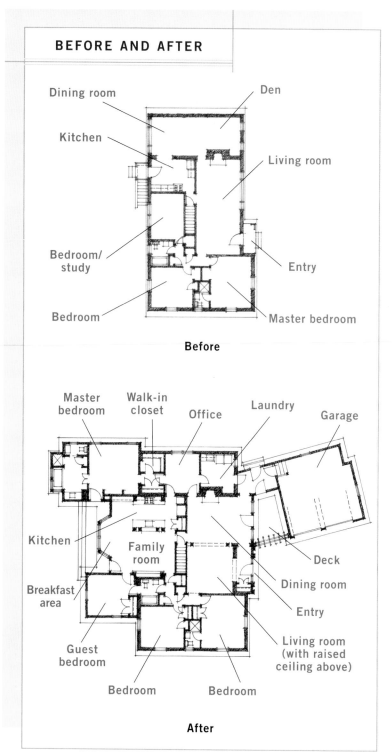

**Before**

Dining room
Den
Kitchen
Living room
Bedroom/study
Entry
Bedroom
Master bedroom

**After**

Master bedroom
Walk-in closet
Office
Laundry
Garage
Kitchen
Family room
Deck
Breakfast area
Dining room
Entry
Guest bedroom
Living room (with raised ceiling above)
Bedroom
Bedroom

the house no longer resembles a shoebox firmly closed with a lid. (Lifting the roof does exciting things for the interior as well, allowing for variation of ceiling heights from room to room.) The new overhang, expressive brackets, and fascia give the house a low-slung, graceful Arts and Crafts look. This imagery is enhanced by the new horizontal wood siding, which has a far less discordant impression than the original compact variegated brick. The horizontal emphasis languidly stretches the home into the landscape.

## New Wings Make the House Fly

Adding a guest room, a master suite, and a breakfast room to the rear of the house created 560 sq. ft. more of interior living space, plus a large deck for outdoor dining. The guest room is located far from the hubbub of the living room and family room, though as a practicality, it shares a bathroom with the other bedrooms.

**Understanding proportion** is key to locating major elements such as fireplaces. In this "before" view, the living room seems lopsided, given the juxtaposition of the door and the mantel. The brass hood is too large (and too shiny) for such a low room.

**The new kitchen** is in exactly the same location as the original. With new openings cut into the wall—framed by double columns—and boxed-in beams that create interest in the ceiling, the room is now spacious and integrated into the family room.

**The living room** was enlarged a few feet to create an entry foyer and corridor. Raising the ceiling clearly creates a larger volume, but what really makes the room feel grand is the simplified color scheme. The room is no longer cut in half by a busy wallpaper, and all patterning is confined to the floor plane. The living room's ruby-red Oriental rug visually connects with the red dining room walls, one room "borrowing" space from the other.

Conventional wisdom (and Rob and Linda's project in Maryland) tells us that building a new two-car garage smack-dab in the front yard next to the main entry would totally overwhelm the scale of a house. But then, making a Ranch over into an Arts and Crafts home is not exactly conventional wisdom. Once you start thinking outside the box, there's no telling what good ideas you'll come up with. Instead of detracting from the arrival sequence, the new garage actually clarifies it. Before, no one was sure exactly where the front door was—it was tucked out of sight, hidden by the bedroom projection. Now the spacious new entrance is a comfortable place for introductions and lingering farewells.

Garages today are receiving considerable design attention. Until very recently, if you wanted a garage

**Nary a hint** of Ranch is left in this renovation. Instead, the house looks much like a summer vacation cottage that has matured into a full-fledged residence as each generation added a wing.

door that was sympathetic to the style of your home, it had to be custom-built. Now, there are a wide variety of vendors who specialize in mass-produced style-appropriate doors. The panel doors of this garage have the same detail as the woodwork on the kitchen divider, linking interior design with exterior design. Garage windows are making a comeback as well. The windows above this garage door are very similar to windows over the entry foyer, an element visually linking old and new. No longer is the garage considered an invisible utilitarian container; it is now a full member of the family.

**Admittedly, the original house** wasn't designed with an imaginative mind, but it was well built and provided good bones for the makeover.

# Total Transformation

ABOVE, **The English Arts and Crafts** tradition is an obvious stylistic inspiration for this home and its parklike setting.

FACING PAGE, **Looking at the photo** on p. 166, it's hard to believe that this is the same hallway. The leaded-glass door leads to a powder room and to the basement stair. Both the old and the "new" house used the same materials—wood paneling, plaster walls, and slate floors—but oh, what a difference detail makes.

W HEN LIZ AND BOB READ the real-estate ad for an open house for a solidly built brick Ranch on two acres that backed up onto a golf course, they rushed out of their house so fast they almost forgot to close the door. When they arrived, they couldn't believe their eyes. "Solidly built" was obviously a polite euphemism for a fortress. Only the sidelight windows were visible from the street, and an ominous Cyclops of a skylight hunkered in the center of the low roof of the massive brick Ranch. The fascia board was so large and the brick so dark that the entire front elevation disappeared in the shadow.

Spurred on by curiosity, they ventured inside. Once they got over their initial reaction to the brutal massing and commercial styling of the house, they recognized that it was very well constructed, the floor plan was well thought out, and the site planning took full advantage of the beautiful setting. The house had definite possibilities.

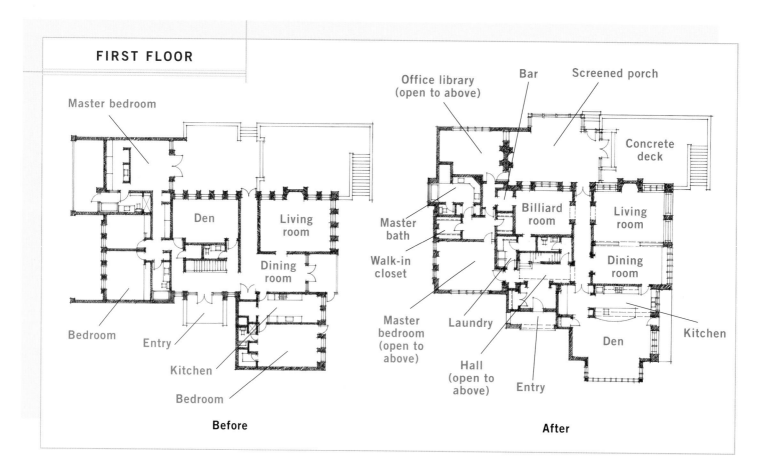

**Before**

**After**

**Slate floors and oak paneling** are evidence that the original home was constructed with quality materials. The vertical paneling was replaced with wainscoting, while the slate floors remain.

# What Goes? What Stays?

When Mark Melaragno of Melaragno Design-Build looked at the house, he agreed with the couple on all counts. After a thorough inspection, he assured them that the foundation would support a second story—it's safe to say that the house was built like a tank. Mark pointed out some elements that they should integrate into the remodel to save costs: the full-wall fireplace, slate floors in excellent condition, and walls constructed of metal-and-lath plaster, not drywall. The basement stair was centrally located, which would work well in laying out a proposed second floor. The powder room was convenient for guests. The basement, with a two-and-a-half-car garage, was in great shape and didn't need any work.

**So many new** homes are built with very tall ceilings, but to no effect. This home office takes advantage of the extra ceiling height to house the family's library. An interesting feature is that the ceiling trim also doubles as a baseboard.

## Back to the (History) Books

Many designers play off the idea that opposites attract. The original house was low, dark, and massive. The new house is tall, light, and sculptural, and even though it reaches back to the previous century for its inspiration, it is strikingly modern in its form. The white stucco is much better suited to reflecting the heat of North Carolina's warm summers than the original dark brick, which absorbs and retains heat. The large arched window in the double-height master bedroom (see the photo on p. 168) is reminiscent of a detail early-20th-century English architect Edwin Lutyens used in his design of two-story living rooms, or "halls" as they were then called.

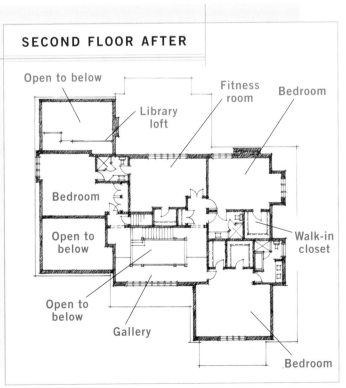

**SECOND FLOOR AFTER**

Open to below

Library loft

Fitness room

Bedroom

Bedroom

Open to below

Walk-in closet

Open to below

Gallery

Bedroom

**Folding interior shutters** are a delightful solution for this oversize arched window. Privacy is gained without losing daylight.

This updated Ranch put a little "English" on the rec room, creating an elegant pub atmosphere, complete with boxed wood beams and a side rail that safely holds refreshments away from the cues.

## Different Decade, Changing Priorities

Bedrooms in 1960s Ranches were small and functional, often with built-in dressers and vanities. Today, we want large rooms, walk-in closets, and our own bathrooms. This house originally had three family bedrooms and two full baths. The fourth bedroom, a maid's room with its own entry and bath, was located off the kitchen. Bob and Liz don't need a live-in maid, but they did want to expand the galley-sized kitchen. Knocking out the wall between the maid's room and the kitchen, spanning the opening with an arched truss, and adding a new bay window bumped out the new kitchen and family room just enough so they are open and inviting. The new window works wonders for the outside elevation as well.

At some future time after the kids have moved out, an elderly parent (or two) might move in with Bob and Liz. The couple specifically requested that the first-floor master suite be oversized to accommodate a sitting room within the bedroom. If parents move in, Liz and Bob will move to one of the bedrooms on the new second floor. The three upstairs bedrooms are organized around a central stair and a light-filled gallery space. No bedroom door is next to another one, so everyone has the comfort of privacy.

A full array of drawers and cabinets in differing sizes below the granite top of the kitchen island does away with the need for hanging cabinets. The arched opening defines the kitchen and family room without isolating one from the other.

RIGHT, **A place for** everything and everything in its place. The depth of this window seat is just the right dimension for the sweater drawers tucked under the cushion. Trophies shine on top of the extra-deep window molding, and the miniature doll collection is shown off to its best advantage in child-scaled glass cabinets.

BELOW, **Gracious stair landings** have a way of becoming children's favorite play places. Safe behind the tripled-up banisters, they can peek down at grownup gatherings and be part of festivities without being in the way.

## Learning from Lutyens

Lutyens emphasized that the exterior and interior of a house should resemble each other. As we have seen, the new exterior is expressed by simple geometric forms interrupted only by the use of warm wood in an ornamental manner. The same holds true for the interior. Throughout the first floor, white is the prevailing color scheme, and wood is used for railings, floors, trim pieces, cabinetry, and beams. In the private rooms, the woodwork is painted white, and the color choices show each family member's preferences. And, in a nod to North Carolina vernacular, the inside-outside connection is in the form of a pine-wood porch that is a delightful three-season room.

In its previous life, this glassed-in porch was merely a concrete patio outside the master bedroom. Cutting brick pavers into the concrete is a relatively inexpensive way to transform dull concrete into a "carpet." During the summer months, the glass panels in the doors can be replaced with screens. Ceiling fans circulate the air, and the recessed ceiling lighting allows bridge parties to continue late into the night.

# Cool and Deliberate

ABOVE, **Nowadays, most dining rooms** (if they exist at all) do double duty. When formal meals are not being served, this room with its cozy seating becomes a combination library and parlor.

FACING PAGE, **The asymmetry** of the elevation tells us that this is a contemporary home, not a weak copy of historic architecture. Good design speaks of its own time and utilizes contemporary building methods and materials.

**W**HEN ATLANTA ARCHITECT Frederick Spitzmiller came across this low-slung Ranch, what excited him wasn't the house but the neighborhood— a charming older garden suburb in Atlanta where most of the homes date from the 1930s. This particular Ranch was in good condition, though it and the few other Ranches in the neighborhood stood out in stark contrast to the peaked roofs and whimsical oddities of the surrounding one-and-a-half- and two-story homes. Rick began to be intrigued by the idea of renovating the house to look as old or older than the houses around it on the exterior and updating the interior with a more airy and cordial interior for space and entertaining.

Rick began the project by analyzing the floor plan. The interior of the Ranch was chopped up by corridors, which meant that the rooms didn't flow into one another. The bedroom wing needed only minor modifications, namely, new windows and improved access to the bathroom. The den was so deep that even the window wall could not bring in enough daylight. The dated feature of a combined living room with a dining alcove was no longer an attraction, and the kitchen was an unfriendly dark, long, and narrow room. Ironically,

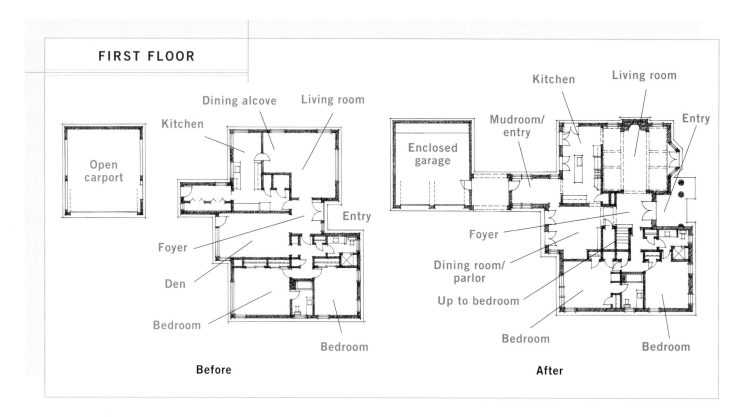

**Before**

Open carport

Kitchen

Dining alcove

Living room

Foyer

Den

Bedroom

Entry

Bedroom

**After**

Enclosed garage

Mudroom/ entry

Kitchen

Living room

Entry

Foyer

Dining room/ parlor

Up to bedroom

Bedroom

Bedroom

**The plain and serviceable** Ranch did not fit into its location in a garden suburb of Atlanta. A total makeover made the house a much better neighbor and likely improved property values.

Rick realized that the defects of the present plan would allow him to do many of the things he wanted to.

## Borrowing to Add Interest

By "borrowing" space from one room to enhance another, Rick was able to accomplish many of his goals. The dimensions of the long, deep den were reduced, creating perfect proportions for a parlor that doubles as a dining room and a library, adjacent to both the patio and the newly configured kitchen. The parlor carved out several feet from the second bedroom for built-in bookshelves. The unwanted dining ell and two awkwardly placed hall closets were divvied up between the kitchen and the living room to create well-proportioned rooms. All these alterations were made without significant structural changes to load-bearing walls.

Exterior doors are often less expensive than windows. Rick took advantage of this to open up the parlor, kitchen, and living room from floor to ceiling by replacing many of the existing windows with double French doors. Paradoxically, the home now has a much stronger connection with the outdoor terraces than when it was stylistically a Ranch.

## Taking a Big Step

Locating a new stair in an existing floor plan takes up a lot more room than most people realize, especially if you want the stair to be a major focal point. One critical element of stair design is head clearance, and once again a shortfall of the original home made a positive design change possible. The old roof needed to be replaced, and Rick took the opportunity to raise the roof. The new pitched roof allows a 13-ft. ceiling height at the entry. This vertical emphasis visually increases the prominence and formality of the entrance sequence.

**The best residential** outdoor spaces have a direct connection to the kitchen, are about the size of a dining room, and incorporate walls for privacy. This "court" has it all: convenience, scale, and character.

## Getting Up to the Attic

**MANY RANCHES** are framed with roof trusses that fill the entire attic void and make it impossible to harvest the space. On the other hand, conventional roof framing, scissor trusses, or roof structures that spring from a knee wall can allow room for colonizing. Add some well-placed dormers or skylights, and the attic space can be yours.

But getting up to that space will be a real challenge to your designer and to your open Ranch plan. Many Ranch attics have access panels to telescoping ship ladders, but typically these are too steep to be made permanent, and they are located in the middle of an already tight corridor. If you're lucky, your Ranch will have an enclosed basement stair that can be structurally, functionally, and visually "extruded" up into a new second floor.

If there's no way to enclose the stair, consider showing it off. Subject to the requirements of your plan and the building code, an exposed open stair in sleek metal or warm wood can be the perfect complement to an expanded modern Ranch.

The story-and-a-half living room receives light from the roof dormer, which bestows the cozy room with a sense of expansive living space. The sloped walls of the ceiling form a delightful "hat" capping the centerpiece postbellum fireplace.

## Combining Dollars and Sense

One advantage architects and other design professionals have over the typical homeowner is that thinking in plan, section, and elevation simultaneously is as natural to them as breathing. So as Rick was redesigning the floor plan, he was also visualizing raising the roof and thinking about how those two decisions would affect the appearance of the exterior of the house. This integrative thinking process is what keeps the end product from looking like three different houses. The original house and landscape were not welcoming. In the

Many homes built after the Civil War in the North and in the South included a wreath motif over the fireplace or the front door as a reminder of all the lives lost in battle. The use of such subtle symbolism in contemporary construction enriches our connection with the past.

ABOVE, **In every house,** one crucial decision can make or break the project. This elegant stair, with turned balusters and banister and beautifully detailed treads, erases any memory that the house was once a plain and ordinary Ranch.

LEFT AND FACING PAGE, **The cheery painted kitchen** gets right down to the business of entertainment, with lots of work spaces that double as buffets, multiple sinks convenient for both cook and bartender, and hanging cabinets that keep the sight lines open so the cook can see whose glass or plate needs refilling.

makeover, the twin chimneys, double-hung windows and French doors, the symmetrical contemporary interpretation of a Palladian entrance, and the cheerful whitewashed brick all give a familiar message of home.

No matter how large or small the budget, keeping costs down is something almost everyone is interested in. Even though this was an extensive project, every dollar was spent to achieve maximum effect, and Rick understood like any other homeowner that trade-offs were necessary. The kitchen is smart and up-to-date, but because collecting cars is more important to Rick than collecting copper pots, he opted to design a comfortable and practical kitchen that counts on its details, rather than expensive finishes, to give it that special look. Entertaining is high on his list, so he made sure that the work counter would double as a buffet when the party spills out to the terrace through the French doors.

## Practical Connections

As much as we might try to deny it, day to day most of us are backdoor sort of folks. Guests and the mail carriers see the front door more often than families do. Instead of continuing the pretense, architects are now recognizing that the lowly mudroom is worthy of a second look. No longer just a place to hang coats and dump sports equipment, the mudroom is a must-have item. In Rick's home, the slate floors of the mudroom are attractive, durable, and easy to clean. The closets, which were really just catchalls for junk, were eliminated, replaced by cheery windows and a small writing table, intentionally too small to attract clutter (see the photo on p. 176).

# Making the Headlines

ABOVE, **The radical makeover** of this Chicago split-level ranch has been variously labeled a boat at sea, a butterfly, an upside-down house, a Cubist sculpture, and an Abstract Expressionist painting, but one no calls it a Ranch anymore. And the interesting color scheme proves that opposites attract: The yellow designates communal rooms and the purple is for family rooms.

FACING PAGE, **Irregular geometry** and sharp angles don't always create a feeling of dissonance, as evidenced by this calm and soothing dining room. The skylights bring in natural light, leaving the substantial uninterrupted wall space for display of the owners' art collection and for a large fireplace.

P ROSPECT HEIGHTS, A SUBURB OF CHICAGO, may seem an unlikely place for architectural critics to flock to. But all that changed when Andrew and Aleksandra gave architect Doug Garofalo the go-ahead for his proposal for a complete makeover of their 1960s split-level Ranch. The house, dubbed by one critic a "Cubist's interpretation of the House of Seven Gables," has attracted a lot of attention.

What was all the brouhaha about? For starters, the clients, both European born, didn't have any sentimental memories attaching them to familiar Midwestern housing styles. An earlier, more conventional addition had added necessary extra square footage, but the homeowners craved more: They wanted excitement and visual interest. They sought Doug out because of his growing reputation as an innovator who approaches the most banal suburban house as a potential laboratory for spatial investigation.

## Everything Old Is New Again

Conventional circumstances prompted the unconventional design. The couple was expecting their second child, and, financially, it made more sense to add on to their home than build new. What they wanted was not

**The catwalk that connects** two second-floor bedrooms called for an all-star cast of trades: welders for the space truss, a steel fabricator for the metal-and-screen banister, glaziers for the glass floor and windows, and the usual cast of painters, tile setters, and finish carpenters.

unusual—another bedroom, a family room, a playroom, and a home office. But the spark that ignited the design was the homeowners' desire for the house to sparkle, with light and new ideas.

With its folded roof plates, ramps, and slipping and sliding walls, the house is reminiscent of the Expressionist architecture movement of the early 1900s (growing up in Europe, the couple were more familiar with this style than with Georgian or Colonial architecture). As a style, Expressionism can be difficult to communicate in drawings because of the dynamic interplay of solid geometries. However, with computer software, particularly animation programs or "fly-throughs," designers can "move" clients through a design in a far more realistic way than drawings or models can portray.

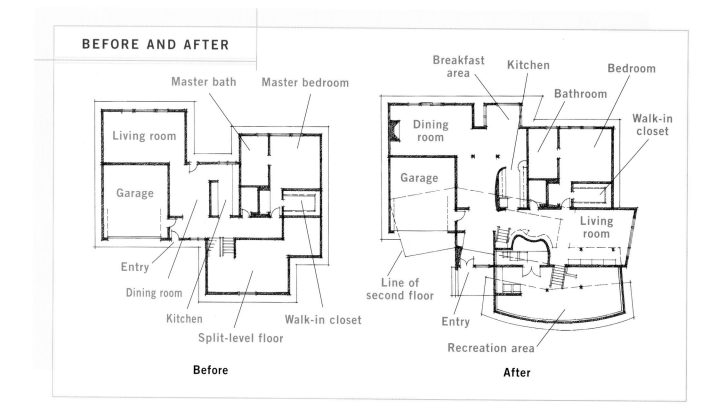

**BEFORE AND AFTER**

Before

Master bath
Master bedroom
Living room
Garage
Entry
Dining room
Kitchen
Split-level floor
Walk-in closet

After

Breakfast area
Kitchen
Bedroom
Bathroom
Dining room
Walk-in closet
Garage
Living room
Line of second floor
Entry
Recreation area

**The twin gables** are about all that is left from the previous house, and even they were an addition to the original. The owners started this project because the house was too dark and boring. The skylights that peek through the center of the roof bring in light to solve the darkness problem, and from the general response, geometry is a cure for boredom.

## How Weird Is It?

The wonderful thing about this house is that it is innovative without being weird. It is exciting, but like all good residential design, it does not overwhelm the personalities of the family members who live in it. The new geometry takes advantage of views and sunlight, a tried-and-true design approach. Off-the-floor, not custom-built furniture, fits comfortably in all the rooms. The kids have generous storage space for their clothes, toys, and books and room to play in their bedrooms. The blue-glass-and-tile bathroom tips its hat to classic '50s Ranch styling, and the kitchen is a modest galley where peanut-butter-and-jelly sandwiches are much more at home than freeze-dried space food.

## Unique Finishes Don't Cost a Fortune

Many homeowners shy away from contemporary design, thinking that if they veer from standard details and finishes, costs will gallop way out of control. But this doesn't have to be the case. One way Aleksandra

**Interesting details** don't necessarily cost more than standard details. In this girl's bedroom, door pulls and handles are replaced with simple cutouts, which create a decorative pattern on the purple storage wall and are easy for small hands to grasp. The dual springing tubular handrails are a joyful alternative to the clunky wood detailing of most children's loft spaces.

LEFT, **Typically, every party** ends up in the kitchen, but this kitchen knows its place. Trimmed down, spare, and no-nonsense, it brings the party into the dynamic public rooms of the house.

FACING PAGE, **Imported from Finland,** the prefinished floor is made from thin slices of end-grain plywood. The thin lines that run consistently through the floor form an interesting striated pattern.

# Ranch Siding: Changing Your Stripes

**WHILE WE ALL** know a tiger can't change its stripes, a Ranch has options and reasons for altering its appearance. The siding material may have been poorly maintained or damaged, or it may simply have worn out; it may have lost its visual appeal or need to bridge the gap between a new addition and the old with a suitable material.

Whatever the reason, it's important to carefully analyze the impact that a change of siding will have on the whole house. A well-designed ranch has a small palette of exterior materials working sympathetically to achieve a coherent whole. This palette includes siding, accented with a masonry material, punctuated by extensive glazing on the backyard side and further brought together by a continuous band of roof with overhang.

New or replacement siding can replicate the original look with horizontal or vertical siding made of wood or woodlike composites. Masonry should mirror or complement the existing masonry unless it replaces that accent. Exterior Insulated Foam Systems (EIFS) provide the opportunity to reintroduce stuccolike finishes in myriad colors while improving the energy efficiency of your home. The use of metal and plastics should be weighed against appearance and life-cycle or long-range costs. Replacing the siding also offers a good opportunity to add or upgrade insulation to reduce energy costs.

and Andrew were able to save thousands of dollars was by looking at the specs and then trying to find a comparable or better product than the one specified for a lower price. For example, instead of using a national manufacturer for their glass ceiling, they found a small company in neighboring Wisconsin that makes a similar product for 25 percent less. And by switching from a Swedish prefinished wood floor to a Finnish prefinished floor, they were able to save 50 percent on the flooring costs.

Garofalo has been quoted several times as saying that now that suburbs are more diverse in their demographics, the way houses look will begin to reflect that change. We think the definition of "different" has changed tremendously since the original Ranches were built. And in this case, different is delightful. If you go back to chapter 1, you will be reminded that this house is carrying on the tradition started in the early days of the Ranch.

# NEW RANCHES

ABOVE, **Winter comes early** (and stays late) in Wisconsin. Interior lighting designed in concert with exterior lighting creates a home that is a glowing refuge, even on the shortest days.

FACING PAGE, **Ranch homes are known** for their indoor-outdoor connections. The back yard of this home connects with a nature preserve, so privacy is at a premium. The deep overhang and energy-efficient windows eliminate the need for heavy draperies.

M OST OF US ASSOCIATE THE RANCH with a distinct historical period, so it may come as a surprise to learn that new Ranch building is very much alive and well. In a 180-degree turn from the popularity of the 1950s expandable home for a growing family, new Ranches are popular with homeowners who want to simplify their lives by downsizing without sacrificing the elegance and quality of life that their larger homes provided. In this final chapter, we'll look at two brand-new Ranches. Although the two architects are a generation apart, both turned to Frank Lloyd Wright for inspiration.

## Why Build New?

For many of us, our home is an extension of our personality; we want to live in a house designed to fit our unique tastes and interests. But why build a new Ranch when there are already so many out there that deserve

**One of the pleasures** of building your own home is that you can build in features that suit your needs. Here, the hallway dimensions were designed specifically to show the owners' art collection from multiple views.

rescuing? There are a number of good reasons. Many of us would rather start fresh than spend time, money, or sweat equity fixing someone else's misadventures. Trying to live through the chaos of a major remodel is no picnic either.

For some homeowners, the Ranch's one-story open plan is the ideal setting for aging in place. And if you build new, not only can accessible design be part of the aesthetic, but all manner of energy-conserving materials and building practices can be integrated into the design. Finally, the Ranch can be as small or as large as you want and still be recognized as a classic American housing type.

## A Modest House

When Chris and Lauren's daughter indicated that she would like to buy her parents' home, the timing couldn't have been better. For some time, the couple had considered downsizing. They no longer needed a large home, and it was becoming inconvenient to go up and down stairs. They wanted a one-story home with a home office, walls designed to exhibit their art collection, and guest rooms to accommodate overnight visits from the grandchildren. While there were plenty of one-story homes in their community to choose from, they really wanted a new home, designed specifically for the way they lived. Friends told them about an available lot directly across from a wildlife preserve. However, when they drove around, there were no empty lots to be seen, though there was one rundown rental property for sale. They met with the realtor, their architect, and their contractor. As soon as the deal was sealed the entire house was torn down, even the foundation, to make way for their new home.

### USONIAN IDEALS

Chris and Lauren chose architect Ken Dahlin and builder Daniel Ward because they admired their previous collaborative efforts. Both architect and builder are influenced by the residential work of Frank Lloyd Wright and other Prairie style architects. All parties quickly agreed that Wright's Usonian home, which influenced the Ranch style, would be an excellent precedent for the couple's home. Wright described the Usonian as "a modest house . . . a dwelling place that has no feeling at all for the 'grand' except as the house extends itself in the flat parallel to the ground." Emulating Wright's process, Ken drew only one plan for the clients' review and worked out details and costs based on that plan.

## MATERIAL MATTERS

This brand-new 2,380-sq.-ft. Ranch pays homage to Wright's work not only in philosophy but also in materials. Wright typically used brick for exterior walls, concrete floors with radiant heating, glass window walls,

**As in any classic** Ranch, the visitor can see all the way through the house from the front door to the backyard. The architect created the Frank Lloyd Wright–inspired etched-glass design to provide privacy for the powder room.

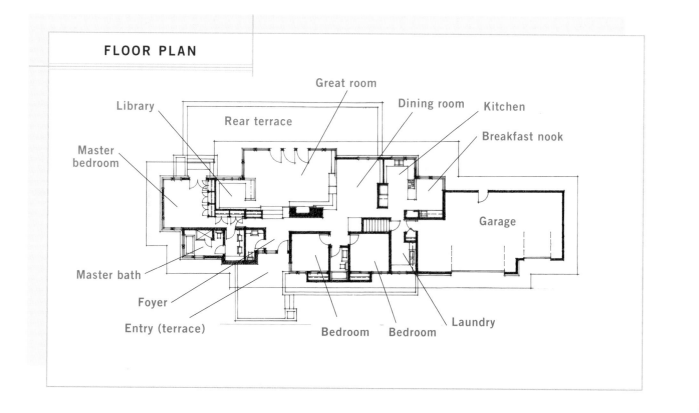

**FLOOR PLAN**

Library
Great room
Rear terrace
Dining room
Kitchen
Breakfast nook
Master bedroom
Garage
Master bath
Foyer
Entry (terrace)
Bedroom
Bedroom
Laundry

## Radiant Floors

**RADIANT HEATING** and concrete floors are gaining in popularity, and while many people think this is new technology, it has been around for 50 years. Why the renewed interest? For a while, homeowners perceived the technology as too expensive and were worried that if something went wrong it would be an expensive fix. The technology has improved, and while the initial costs are high, long-term energy savings and creature comforts are significant. Most importantly more and more contractors have experience installing the system, and it is no longer unusual. There are even new radiant heat systems that can be installed under wood floors. Concrete floors are simply beautiful and easy to maintain.

and wood and plywood for the other walls, and this design follows suit. When the Roman brick the architect specified proved too costly, Chris and Lauren switched to a standard size, but they were adamant that the color choice remain. The architect and contractor located the last batch of brick produced in the special color "greige."

Windows are a very important feature of this Ranch. The unique corner butt-jointed windows are not glass but a very thick, transparent energy-efficient fusion of acrylics, is similar to aquarium glass in strength. The windows "disappear" at the corner, giving the illusion that the cantilevered roof floats over the window wall without support.

Throughout the house, great care is taken to create a sense of connectedness from one room to another and to the outdoors. The architect used interior glass partitions between the walls and ceilings, to heighten the open feeling. Glass can bounce noise but because the house is built for a couple, this is not a major concern.

### UNDER ONE ROOF

One of Wright's favorite quotes is from *The Book of Tea*: "The reality of a room is to be found in the space enclosed by the roof and the wall, not in the roof and walls themselves." Lauren and Chris's home takes that philosophy to heart. The brick walls, interior and exterior, support the large roof, gathering as many of the rooms as possible under one ceiling. Folding and unfolding ceiling planes visually connect all the major rooms, and the spotlights dance around the ceiling like stars in the sky. Horizontal bands of warm maple define an intimately scaled 7-ft. wall height without interrupting the overhead flow of light and space shaped by the

ABOVE, **Concrete floors with** or with-out radiant heating are easy to main-tain and are as popular now as they were in the 1950s. The bathroom floors and the front entry hall of this home are also warmed by radiant heat, eliminating the need for bulky or unsightly radiators.

LEFT, **The frameless windows** allow the view of the backyard to flow directly into the kitchen. An abundance of under-the-counter storage does away with overhead cabinets.

**In lieu of** a walk-in closet, this house has a walk-by closet. Even in a house for two, bedrooms need interior walls for privacy, and this bedroom corridor to the master bath is lined with closets.

10-ft. ceilings. The brick fireplace wall appears to be the major structural element holding up the ceiling, while the walls, floors, and roof are treated simply as enclosing screens, parallel planes that move through space. The underside of the eave, the ceiling soffit, is intended to be visible from the interior.

At night, interior lighting casts a reflection on the underside of the soffit, creating a glowing perimeter around the house and extending the house out into the night landscape. During the day the cantilever of the roof acts as a light diffuser, shielding large window walls from too much glare.

# The Overhang

**THE ROOF OVERHANG** is as important a part of the Ranch as white Stetsons were to the heroes in those Saturday serials we used to watch in our Ranch TV room. The overhang adds horizontal heft to the Ranch as it connects the house to its site, and it ties together the other architectural elements with strong shadow lines that give visual distinction to the Ranch home. This overhang also protects the perimeter from the major onslaughts of weather, while trapping many a far-flung Frisbee.

But there's more to it than that. On a scale much larger than any new sustainable gadget, the Ranch overhang provides suburban American homeowners with one of the most successful and useful passive daylighting devices ever. *Daylighting* is a modern-day description for something as old as the sun—designing to maximize the sun's contribution to the enjoyment of your home.

The overhang is an extension of the roof that is meant to shield the windows in summer and expose them in winter, and consequently yield energy savings throughout the year. In summer, the Ranch overhang provides shade from the high

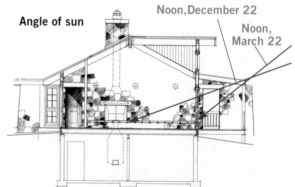

**Angle of sun**

Noon, December 22

Noon, March 22

60-degree angle of the summer sun, but in winter, when the sun angle is lower, the overhang allows the sun to enter the glazing and warm the interior space. Linear radiators at the glazing sill line, coupled with insulated draperies, can seal the heat within and prevent heat from radiating out of the space at night.

**Taking a page** from earlier Ranch design, the overhang of this brand-new Ranch eliminates the need for gutters, creating a cleaner roof line. The deep overhang also provides shelter from the elements at the entryways—not to mention that the windows are shielded from rain and snow.

## Belonging to the Land

When we first spoke to Al and his wife, Dawn, about their plans for a new home, it was evident that Al knew (and loved) every inch of the beautiful property that his family had owned for over 100 years. Dawn was intrigued by the message of Sarah Susanka's *The Not So Big House* that bigger homes are not necessarily better. The house was to be for just the two of them and their dog, Ruffian (who got her own dog condo off the garage).

Al and Dawn were fairly flexible about the style of the house, but they knew exactly what they wanted when it came to specifics—right down to the bathroom hardware. Because the land was so important to them, they were equally specific about site concerns. They didn't want the house to be visible from the road, even in winter; they were adamant that the existing mature forest must be respected; and they wanted as many different views as possible from within the home. It was also important to have as many direct connections with the outdoors as possible.

ABOVE, **Taking cues** (and stones) from the landscape, local materials were used to blend this new Ranch into its surroundings. The stone comes from a quarry 30 miles away, as well as from the site excavation. During the excavation of the foundation, stones from the site were gathered and stockpiled for use in the landscape. The understated gray board-and-batten exterior matches the bark of native trees.

RIGHT, **Ranch hallmarks** march right into the new century: Stone walls link inside and outside, and the use of glass allows the garden to be viewed as a feature from both inside and outside the house.

## THE LEAF AND THE HAND

As we walked the 250-acre site, in an ancient landscape of rolling hills, deep ravines, and abundant rock, we picked up various artifacts along the way—a turkey feather, an oak leaf, some lichen, several stones of varied hues—all of which gave us clues for the architectural concept, colors, and materials for the finished house.

The gray paint color came from the turkey feather, the stone walls of the house literally rise from the site, and there was no doubt that the house would incorporate wood. To start the dialogue with Al and Dawn, we showed them a diagram we had sketched on a site visit—a hand superimposed on an oak leaf. Our suggestion, one remembered from the teachings of Frank Lloyd Wright, was that the house should extend into the landscape rather than sit on top of it. Each "finger," or "lobe," would direct their view over the open farm fields, down a wooded ravine, or up a rolling hill. Then, out of the magnificent 250 acres, we had to narrow

**In contrast to** the soaring exposed wood ceilings of the great room, the bedroom ceiling is conventional height, creating a cozy scale. Exterior lighting ensures that the night view is as spectacular as the daylight vista.

down the location to one that met their criteria. It was easier than we thought. The "perfect" site presented itself. Three landscapes—ravine, woods, and farm fields—were all visible from a slight rise, and no healthy large trees would have to be removed.

The idea of capturing distinct views extended to outdoor living as well. Several different porches provide an additional 250 sq. ft. of living space. The screened porch conveniently located off the kitchen faces south, just right for twilight dining. The fireplace allows conversation to continue late into the night (even summer nights in Wisconsin can be cool enough for a fire). From the porch connected to the great room there is a filtered view of a farm field, which is still worked.

## FLOOR PLAN

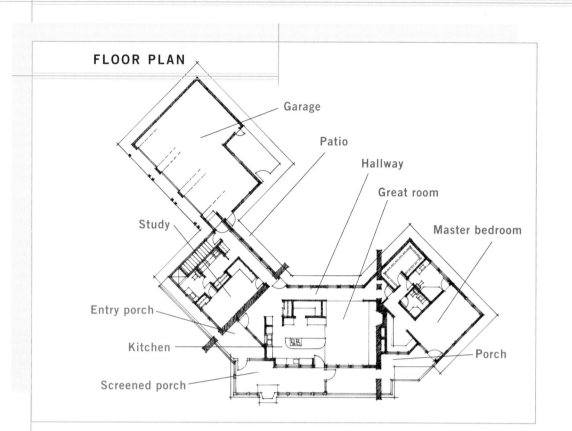

- Garage
- Patio
- Hallway
- Great room
- Master bedroom
- Study
- Entry porch
- Kitchen
- Screened porch
- Porch

FACING PAGE, **The wood-work in the kitchen** melds nicely with the great room, and all hardware is hidden—no exposed knobs, handles, or hinges define the cabinetry as utilitarian.

**In the 1950s,** the barbecue pit was a must-have item. This porch fireplace is the 2000s version, close to the kitchen for convenience and screened (even under the floorboards) for comfort.

Protected by a stone wall portal, a private porch leads to the master bedroom, with an eastern view down a steep ravine.

### ALONE AND TOGETHER

One of the challenges of designing a small, 2,220-sq.-ft. house miles from the nearest village is to create intimacy without fostering claustrophobia. The bending of the plan to capture different views also enabled us to provide an open plan for the living/dining/kitchen area, while one "lobe" became the master bedroom suite, his-and-her baths, a shared walk-in closet, and an alcove, and the other "lobe" holds the study, guest bath, and utility room.

Most homes shown in this book eliminated corridors, but this house needed one to ensure that the whole "story" of the site is not told at one time. We wanted Al and Dawn to have views to the landscape from the house but not to feel as though they were liv-

ing in a goldfish bowl. Rather than enclose the corridor with floor-to-ceiling walls, we borrowed a page from the built-in storage systems of the 1950s Ranch. Our 21st-century kitchen/corridor built-in houses the coat closet for the front entry, the pantry for the kitchen, bookshelves for the living room, and an art wall on the corridor. It's a room within a room.

## CUSTOM DESIGN AND RESALE APPEAL

Al and Dawn intend this to be the last home they build, but just in case they do end up moving, they

included some flexibility in the floor plan so more bedrooms could be added and the house would appeal to larger families. A full basement with tall ceilings and stubbed-in plumbing for a future bathroom was part of the original program. Since the basement windows were large enough to meet Wisconsin's code requirements for bedrooms, both the exercise room and the north wing could be converted into large light-filled bedrooms and meet the original criteria that every room have a great view. Interestingly, this is a U-turn from Ranch construction in the 1950s, when some Ranch owners started out

**While dormers are not** a traditional Ranch feature, the high windows bring in light that plays across the planes of the exposed pine ceiling. Doubled-up laminated beams reinforce the idea that the roof "springs" from the walls.

living in a finished basement as they built the rest of the house above them.

When they first reviewed the drawings, Al and Dawn were surprised to see the vaulted exposed wood ceiling supported by wood lams and two massive stone walls. They hadn't envisioned anything other than conventional drywall ceilings and walls. It took a while, but working closely with the contractor, we were able to convince them that expressing these two materials in the great room would connect the house to the landscape in a meaningful way and make a small home sumptuous. Now Al and Dawn say they can't imagine why they hesitated.

## The Ranch Rides Again

Slowly, people are beginning to realize that the Ranch never went away because it is the all-American housing style. Almost everyone we know has lived in a Ranch at one time or another. Ranch living space values the free, flexible, and spontaneous way we really live, without fussy detail, excess square footage, or elaborate finishes. The Ranch has not only survived, it is on its way to becoming timeless. Frank Lloyd Wright's quote about one of his dusted-off projects sums up the appeal of the Ranch: "It was a good plan then, and now 50 years later, it is still a perfectly good plan."

Well built and connected to the landscape, Ranch homes are so numerous that in most communities they are one of the most affordable housing styles. The homes in this book show that with an active imagination, a little self-control, and a critical eye for opportunity, the Ranch could be the home of your future and of your dreams.

TOP, **Local materials** and local talent built this home. In Wisconsin there is a tradition that stonemasons sign walls that they are particularly proud of. This wall bears their signature.

ABOVE, **One big porch** makes sense if you have a large family, but several small porches of different character add variety and intimacy in a house for two. The porch off the master bedroom is the perfect place for a couple to stargaze.

# Sources

**BOOKS**

For further reading on the history of Ranches and contemporary classics:

May, Cliff. *Western Ranch Houses.* Los Angeles: Hennessey + Ingalls, 1997.

McCoy, Esther. *Case Study Houses: 1945-1962.* Los Angeles: Hennessey + Ingalls, 1977.

Nelson, George. *Living Spaces.* New York: Whitney Publications, 1952.

Sunset Magazine. *Western Ranch Houses.* Los Angeles: Hennessey + Ingalls, 1999.

Wright, Olgivanna Lloyd. *Frank Lloyd Wright: His Life, His Work, His Words.* New York: Horizon, 1966.

For a well-illustrated, clear, and concise description of residential building:

Haun, Larry. *Habitat for Humanity: How to Build a House.* Newtown, CT: The Taunton Press, 2002.

For a well-illustrated, clear, and concise description of the building process:

Ching, Frank. *Building Construction Illustrated.* New York: Van Nostrand Reinhold, 1991.

For a contemporary restating of the programming classic, Christopher Alexander's *A Pattern Language: Towns, Buildings, Construction.* Oxford University Press, 1977.

Jacobson, Max, Silverstein, Murray, and Winslow, Barbara. *Patterns of Home.* Newtown, CT: The Taunton Press, 2002.

**FEATURED DESIGNERS AND ARCHITECTS**

The Architecture Studio (pp. 2,7, 86–93)
Jeffrey Michael Tohl
Los Angeles, CA 90048-4114

August Architects (Vance Cheatham & Karl Hirschman) (pp. i, 27 (bottom), 68–75)
216 North Candler St.
Decatur, GA 30030

Boss & Agnew Architects
(pp. 5, 32 (bottom) 108–115)
P.O. Box 6048
Ketchum, ID 83340

Otis Bradley (pp. 62–67)
911 Montana Ave., Suite F
Santa Monica, CA 90403

Drager Gould Architects
(pp. 13, 34, 78, 127, 146–151)
Old City Hall, Suite 310
Tacoma, WA 98402

Laurence Garrick Associates
(pp. 37–38, 133)
Designing and Planning,
119 East Market
Rhinebeck, NY 12572

Garofalo Architects
(pp. 1, 8, 12, 28, 132,180–185)
3752 North Ashland
Chicago, IL 60613

Genesis Architecture (pp. 16, 186–193)
Ken Dahlin, Architect
4061 N. Main St., Suite 200
Racine, WI 53402-3116

Gerloff Residential Architects (pp.46–53)
4007 Sheridan Avenue, South
Minneapolis, MN 55410

Gill & Gill Architects (p. 129)
Harrison Gill, principal
39 Wall St., Suite # 1
Norwalk, CT 06850

Harwood + Tabberson (pp. 6, 76, 102–107)
2900 W. Torquay Rd.
Muncie, IN 47304-3229

HBF + Architects (pp. 124, 140–145)
H. Bruce Finkelstein, AIA
1777 Reisterstown Rd., Suite 118
Baltimore, MD 21208

McInturff Architects (pp. 9, 30, 39, 54–61)
420 Leeward Place,
Bethesda, MD 20816

Melaragno Design Build
(pp. 125, 164–171)
1641 Brandon Road
Charlotte, NC 28207

Mitchell Architecture (pp. 84, 94–101)
1324 E. Green Meadow Lane
Greenwood Village, CO 80121

Morris-Day Residential Design and Development
(pp. 7, 27 (top), 33, 152–157, 158–163)
Dwight McNeil, Senior Architect
4620 Lee Hwy., Suite 215
Arlington, VA 22207

Paul Murdoch Architects
(pp.iii, 11, 126 (top) 134–139)
5150 Wilshire Blvd., Suite 504
Los Angeles, CA 90036

SALA Architects, Inc. (pp. 81–83, 116–123)
Tim Fuller, Design Architect
43 Main St., SE, Suite 410
Minneapolis, MN 55414

Scheidegger & Tobias Architecture
(pp. 31, 32 (top), 40–45)
7 Mount Lassen Drive, Suite A-134
San Rafael, CA 94903

Jim Sims, Interior Design (pp. 4, 18–25)
2575 Peachtree Rd., Suite 303
Atlanta, GA 30305

Spitzmiller & Norris
(pp. vi, 29, 79, 131, 172–179)
5825 Glenridge Dr., Building 1, Suite 206
Atlanta, GA 30328

The Architecture Studio, Inc.
Jeffrey Tohl
(pp. ii, 2, 77, 86–93)
8522 West Third Street
Los Angeles, CA 90048

Louis Wasserman & Associates
(pp. ii, 1, 14, 186, 194–199)
828 N. Broadway
Milwaukee, WI 53202

# Index